Take Two Aspirin. . . and Call Me in Hawaii

The World's Best Jokes on Doctors, Health, and Wellness

Take Two Aspirin. . . and Call Me in Hawaii

The World's Best Jokes on Doctors, Health, and Wellness

David McLaughlan

BARBOUR
PUBLISHING

© 2011 by Barbour Publishing, Inc.

ISBN 978-1-61626-253-2

Published by Barbour Publishing, Inc., P.O. Box 719,
Uhrichsville, Ohio 44683 www.barbourbooks.com

*Our mission is to publish and distribute inspirational products
offering exceptional value and biblical encouragement to the masses.*

Member of the
Evangelical Christian
Publishers Association

Printed in the United States of America.

Contents

"You probably came in contact with
someone who has an infectious smile."

Introduction

There's a joke about a man whose doctor tells
him to give up. . .well, all the things he enjoys!
"Will it help me live longer?" he asks. "No," says
the doctor, "it will just seem like it."

There's another, better, way of making
your life seem longer. Fill it with laughter. An
evening spent laughing with friends can seem
longer than mere hours. A morning spent
laughing with children or grandchildren can
seem a heavenly eternity.

More and more these days, people are real-
izing what the wise men of the Bible knew all
along—that laughter might just possibly be
good for you!

"A cheerful heart is good medicine," it says in Proverbs, "but a crushed spirit dries up the bones."

So, we offer you this collection of medical mix-ups and hope you enjoy it—because if your bones dry up you might just find yourself visiting that doc who wants folk to give all the fun stuff up!

"I'm the doctor who brings the cards. I'm a cardiologist."

General Hospital

Hospitals are like miniature (and sometimes not-so-miniature) versions of our own lives. Birth and death are there and everything in between. Everyone in the hospital is there either to help or be helped, just as in the wider world, but (just as in the wider world) so much other stuff gets in the way, and the end result can be chaotic.

Here are some of the things that help make it all go terribly, funnily wrong and prove that the command to "love one another" is no easier to carry out in a hospital than it is in everyday life.

Say What?

The nurse's curiosity got the better of her. She'd read the heavily bandaged patient's chart but couldn't imagine how he got those injuries—so she asked.

Even through his bandages she could tell he was embarrassed.

"Well, ma'am," he started, "I was on one of them roller coasters. And this one went hundreds of feet high. Each time we reached the highest point, just before we started going down again I saw a sign overhead. But I'm a little shortsighted, so next time I came by I stood up to read it. It smacked me on the head and over the side I went."

"Oh my goodness," gasped the nurse. "And did you get to read what the sign said before you fell?"

"Yes," he sighed. "It said, 'Remain seated at all times.'"

And No, He Doesn't Dissect Oranges

An elderly lady was sitting in the hospital waiting room. Getting a bit bored, she struck up a conversation with a vaguely medical-looking gentleman who just happened to be passing by.

After he assured her he knew nothing of her case she asked, "And what is it you do here?"

"Oh I don't work here, ma'am," he said. "I'm a naval surgeon."

"Oh my," she said, a little scornfully. "Haven't we gotten fancy these days with all our specializations? In my day a surgeon would operate on any part of you!"

Here's an Eye-dea

A surgeon worked in the country's foremost eye hospital, and he considered himself the best surgeon there. To improve his reputation even further, he came up with a radical procedure for restoring sight to the blind.

With his trial patient under anesthetic he basically stripped her eyes down into their component segments and rebuilt them so they worked. The procedure was a success, the patient was subjected to all kinds of tests, and he wrote the event up in a professional journal. Only then did he discover there was a problem.

The patient could see well enough to thread a needle, but she was completely unable to distinguish one letter from another. More tests were carried out. Her brain was examined. Eventually the surgeon put his pride aside and consulted with his peers. No one could find the answer.

Finally, a nurse suggested she might have

the answer. The surgeon sneered at the very idea!

"How long has she been blind?" the nurse asked.

"All her life!" the surgeon barked. "That's what makes my success so amazing and this problem so frustrating!"

"So. . . ," the nurse tried hard to keep a straight face. "She never learned to read then."

Practice Makes Perfect

The cheery young nurse was doing early-morning rounds.

"Good morning, Mr. Hackensack," she said. "Your cough sounds much better this morning!"

"Yes," said Hackensack wearily. "That's because I've been practicing it all night!"

Be Patient with These Patient Records, Part 1

- By the time he was admitted, his rapid heart had stopped, and he was feeling better.
- Patient has chest pain if she lies on her left side for over a year.
- On the second day the knee was better, and on the third day it had completely disappeared.
- Patient was released to outpatient department without dressing.
- The patient is tearful and crying constantly. She also appears to be depressed.
- Discharge status: Alive but without my permission.
- The patient will need disposition, and we will get a doctor to dispose of him.
- He was not to lift or drive his car.
- The patient has no temperature today.
- The patient has a questionable cousin with colitis.
- She was a restrained driver in the backseat.
- The patient is confused, but the family states that she has been intermittently confused for some time and particularly about. . .she has been intermittently,

intermittently been increasingly confused over the last three months.

- He has one brother and two half-female siblings.
- Patient has left white blood cells at another hospital.
- Patient's medical history has been remarkably insignificant with only a forty-pound weight gain in the past three days.
- She is numb from her toes down.
- Patient has two teenage children, but no other abnormalities.

Specific Enough?

A technician was monitoring the telemetry suite of a hospital. One of the screens lit up, and he heard a patient say, "Can you send my nurse in, please? I'm having some pain here."

The tech checked the name of the occupant of that room and activated his microphone, "Can you tell me exactly where you're having that pain, Mr. Miller?"

"Uh, yeah." The voice came back. "In room 221. I'm in bed."

Can You Hear Me, Daddy?

It was "Take Your Child to Work Day," and the doctor had brought his six-year-old daughter to the hospital. He introduced her to everyone, gave her a tour of the building, and then showed her the corner office he worked out of.

He was sure she was impressed by how important her daddy was, and when she picked up his stethoscope he felt a surge of excitement. He had impressed her so much she undoubtedly wanted to be a doctor just like him.

The little girl put the stethoscope to her ears.

As tears of pride came to the doctor's eyes, his daughter lifted the end of the stethoscope to her mouth and said, "Welcome to McDonald's. May I take your order please?"

Hospital Lite

Even hospitals have to move with the times. These days people are more aware of healthy options. Maybe that's why the Mayo Clinic changed its name to the Balsamic Vinaigrette Clinic!

An Aid to Sleep

A man who had just undergone extensive surgery kept complaining about having a bump on his head and a terrible headache.

Because his surgery had been nowhere near his head the nurse was totally confused but did her best.

Later that day she passed the anesthesiologist who had been part of the man's operating team.

"It's the strangest thing." She told him all about the symptoms and asked if he thought it might be psychosomatic or some kind of post-surgery syndrome.

The anesthesiologist blushed.

"No. He really does have a bump on his head, and I'm not surprised he has a headache. You see, halfway through the operation we ran out of anesthetic. . . ."

Be Patient with These Patient Records, Part 2

- The patient had waffles for breakfast and anorexia for lunch.
- The baby was delivered, the cord clamped and cut and handed to the pediatrician, who breathed and cried immediately.
- The patient was in his usual state of good health until his airplane ran out of gas and crashed.
- I saw your patient today, who is still under our car for physical therapy.
- The patient lives at home with his mother, father, and pet turtle, who is presently enrolled in day care three times a week.
- While in the emergency room, she was examined, X-rated, and sent home.
- The skin was moist and dry.
- Patient was alert and unresponsive.
- When she fainted, her eyes rolled around the room.
- Coming from Detroit, this man has no children.

Only Caught in a High, Green Environment

A medical secretary was transcribing recorded notes from a doctor, but one particular bit was puzzling her, so she handed the headphones to her colleague and asked her to listen.

"Wow!" the colleague said, "I never heard of that disease before."

"Me neither," the secretary said. And she typed into the computer, "This man has Pholenfromatry."

Later on she got the chance to ask the doctor what that strange new disease was all about.

He didn't know what she was talking about, so she showed him the note on the computer.

"It's not a new disease," he told her. "It's a very old, very common problem. You see, this man has fallen. . .from. . .a. . .tree."

At Least It Wasn't Crackers

Q. Why did the cookie go to the hospital?
A. It was feeling really crummy!

No, It's Not a Medical Term

Harry was in the hospital recovering after surgery when an attentive nurse asked him how he was feeling.

"Yeah. . . ," he said, a little hesitantly. "I'm okay I guess. I just didn't like what the doctor said during my operation."

"Oh?" said the nurse. "What did he say?"

"Well, he said a four letter word."

"Never!" The nurse was genuinely shocked. "What was it?"

"Oops!"

Allergic to Brains

Part of the hospital's admissions policy meant that patients were asked about any allergies they had. The admissions staff would then write the allergy on a band along with the patient's name before fixing it around the patient's wrist.

It seemed to work well until an extremely irate gentleman marched up to the desk and demanded to know who had been labeling his mother "bananas" without a proper medical examination!

Hey, I Heard That!

Some people claim they can hear what's going on even when they're under anesthetic. Here are just a few of the things you wouldn't want to hear during your operation:

- "Ladies and gentlemen, this will be a learning experience for all of us."
- "Nurse, could you turn to the next page of the instruction manual, please?"
- "Bad dog! Bring that back!"
- "Nobody move! I lost a contact lens!"
- "Nurse, could you hand me the, uh, thingy. . . ."
- "What do you mean he's not insured?"
- "Could somebody stop that from beating? It's putting me off!"

Sleep Tight

A man received a bill for the cost of his operation. He wasn't happy about any of it, but he thought the anesthetist's fee was particularly exorbitant. So, he phoned him up.

"Is this a mistake?" he demanded.

"No, I don't think so," the anesthetist replied. "Why?"

"Because that's a whopping amount of money just for knocking someone out," the man retorted.

"Ah!" that anesthetist said. "You're right. There has been a mistake."

"There has?" said the delighted man.

"Yes," said the anesthetist. "You see, I knock people out for free. The 'whopping amount of money' is for making sure you wake back up again!"

If the Fonz Was a Doctor

Who is the coolest guy in the hospital?

The Ultra Sound Man.

And when he's not there?

The Hip Replacement Guy.

Paging Doctor Bubba

You know you're in a genuine redneck hospital when. . .

- you share a room with a sick cow.
- you get a choice of walking frames— with or without a gun rack.
- the anesthesiologist feeds you clear liquid from a mason jar.
- the ambulance has NASCAR bumper stickers and beer can holders.
- surgical equipment includes dynamite and duct tape.

- they use Chevy hubcaps for bedpans.
- the bill is made up for either dollars or chickens.

What Goes Around. . .

The chief executive of an HMO died and was very relieved that he got into heaven. Of course, he had to check out after forty-eight hours.

Not the Sharpest Instrument

The surgeon asked his patient, "Have you ever undergone surgery here before?"

"Yes," said the patient.

"What for?" asked the surgeon.

"For eight hundred bucks," said the patient.

"But what was the problem?" the surgeon asked.

"I only had six hundred," the patient said.

"No, no," the frustrated surgeon said. "What was your complaint?"

"That your bills are too high!"

Designed by Committee

The hospital's board of directors wanted to add a new wing, but they weren't sure if it was a smart move, given the current financial climate. So they asked all the specialists who might benefit from the new wing what they thought.

- The allergists voted to scratch it.
- The dermatologists advised no rash moves.
- The gastroenterologists had a bad feeling in their gut about it.
- The proctologists said, "We are in arrears."
- The neurologists thought the directors had a lot of nerve.
- The obstetricians said the directors were laboring under a misconception.
- The ophthalmologists considered the idea shortsighted.
- The pathologists yelled, "Over my dead body!"
- The pediatricians said, "Grow up!"
- The psychiatrists thought the whole idea was madness.
- The surgeons washed their hands of the whole thing.
- The radiologists could see right through it.
- The internists thought it was a bitter pill to swallow.
- The plastic surgeons said, "This puts a whole new face on the matter."
- The podiatrists thought it was a step forward.

- The urologists felt the scheme wouldn't hold water.
- The anesthesiologists thought the whole idea was a gas.
- And the cardiologists didn't have the heart to say no.

"We found a bunch of these clogging
your arteries. They're cholesterol pills."

2
The Cure Is Worse Than the Disease

These days we will try any new, usually
expensive, fad to cure symptoms that might
better be addressed by a healthier lifestyle. But
we don't want to hear that! We want our cures
to be mysterious and wonderful—preferably
involving as little effort as possible.

These wonderful bodies God gave us will
usually work just fine, left to their own devices,
but when things start to go wrong, that's when

we reach out for the latest remedy.

The cures mankind has tried over the centuries would make your hair stand on end! Uh. . .usually not the hair restorers, though!

A Dry Sense of Humor

A man went to his doctor and told him that he hadn't been feeling well lately. The doctor examined the man, left the room, and came back with three different bottles of pills.

"Take the green pill with a big glass of water when you wake up," he said. "Take the blue pill with a big glass of water after you eat lunch. Then just before going to bed take the red pill with another big glass of water."

Startled to be put on so much medicine the man said, "Oh, Doc! Now you got me worried! Exactly what is my problem?"

The doctor replied, "You're not drinking enough water."

If I Can't Cure You of That. . .

Jim was feeling really awful, so he decided to visit the doctor. The doc prescribed some pills, and Jim took them faithfully. But he didn't feel any better, so he went back. The doc examined him again, gave him a shot, and told Jim he would be better by morning. But when the morning came Jim still felt awful.

The doc decided a patch might help. It didn't.

Frustrated and embarrassed the doc told Jim to go home, take a bath with his clothes on, and then go for a walk after dark.

"Doc!" Jim protested. "If I do that at this time of year I'll catch pneumonia!"

"Exactly," the doc shouted. "And I know how to cure pneumonia!"

Drowning, a Good Cure for Indigestion

A man went to see his doctor about some stomach problems he had. The doctor advised drinking warm, salty water at least an hour before breakfast.

The next week he came back to the doctor's office.

"Did you drink the warm, salty water an hour before breakfast?" the doctor asked.

"Gee, Doc," the man replied. "I really tried, but fifteen minutes of the stuff was the most I could manage!"

Maybe He Should've Said Please

A man parks in front of a pharmacist's store and runs in.

"Quick," he says. "I need something to cure a serious case of hiccups!"

The pharmacist leans over the counter and slaps him hard on the cheek.

"What. . . ," the man splutters. "What on earth. . . ?"

"Well," the pharmacist says, rather smugly, "you don't have the hiccups anymore, do you?"

"No, I don't," the man shouts. "But my wife, who's out in the car, still does!"

A Sure Cure for All Ills

"Take one of these blue pills," the doctor advised his patient. "I've started giving them to everyone for everything."

"What are they?" the patient asked.

"Well now, I'm not really sure," the doctor said.

"But you think they work?"

"Definitely!" the doctor said. "No one ever comes back for more!"

News Flash

Medical researchers have discovered a new disease that has no symptoms. It is impossible to detect, and there is no known cure.

Fortunately no cases have been reported thus far.

Dough!

A mother complained to her doctor about her daughter's strange eating habits. "She just lies in bed all day eating yeast and car wax. I'm worried about what's going to happen to her."

"Don't worry," said the doctor. "One of these days she'll rise and shine."

A Nice Looooooong Bath

Sam met Britney in town and noticed she was really suffering from a bad cold.

"Have you seen a doctor about that cold?" he asked.

"Well, I probably should," Britney said. "Can you recommend somebody good?"

So Sam gave Britney the number of his own doctor.

A week later they met again.

"How did it go with the doctor?" he asked.

"Oh, cool," Britney replied. "He gave me some medicine to drink immediately after a hot bath."

"Did it work?" Sam asked. "Is your cold better?"

"Well, I don't know, silly," Britney replied. "I haven't finished drinking the bath yet!"

Bet He Still Billed

Zack and Joe were going to town on doctors. Zack had had some awful experiences and didn't think any doctors were any good. Joe generally agreed, but there was one exception.

"Doc Brown, though," he said, "he's something else!"

"How come?" Zack wanted to know.

"Well," said Joe, "I went to Doc Black. He gave me some medicine, and I was awful sick. So, I went to Doc White. He gave me a different medicine, and I reckoned I was drawing my last breaths. My wife phoned Doc Brown. He was too busy playing golf to come. I reckon he saved my life!"

A Bigger Pill to Swallow

A man hobbled into the hospital and asked for his foot to be x-rayed. Having discovered it wasn't broken, they took him back to the waiting area. A doctor came over and handed him a surprisingly large pill.

Just then an emergency case came in, and the doc had to see to it.

Sitting there in pain the man looked at the large pill. How on earth was he going to swallow that? But he was in a lot of pain, and he didn't know how long the doc would be. So he closed his eyes and forced himself to swallow it. It tasted disgusting.

Just then the doctor came back with a basin full of hot water.

"Okay," he said. "Just dissolve the pill in the water, and soak your foot in it for a while."

No, Captain, It's a Medical Condition

Buddy was in a real bad way! His eyes bulged out, his face was constantly red, and he had serious trouble breathing. The doctors couldn't do anything for him, and Buddy had convinced himself he was going to die.

So he decided to go out in style. He withdrew all his money from the bank, booked a round-the-world cruise, and bought some expensive new clothes. Deciding he'd better look nice for the dinners on ship he ordered twenty silk shirts.

"Size fourteen," he told the shop assistant.

"You're kidding," said the assistant. "You're much bigger than a fourteen. I'd say you take a size sixteen collar at least."

"Listen, doofus," said Buddy, "I know my sizes."

"It's your call," said the assistant. "But I'm telling you, your eyes are gonna bulge out, and your face is always gonna be red. . . ."

Flat-Out Ill

A man went into the doctor's office for his test results but found it strangely quiet. A nurse in a biohazard suit indicated he should follow her. At the end of the corridor he stepped into a room, and she slammed the door shut behind him.

Looking around in amazement, he was even more startled when a voice spoke to him via an intercom. His doctor informed him that his results showed he had about every infectious disease known to man. He would have to stay in the room.

"Look on the bright side, though," the doctor said. "You'll get pizza and flapjacks every day."

"Cool," the man said. "Will they help me get better?"

"Doubt it," the doctor said, "but they're the only food we can slide under the door!"

Eye Don't Think That's Very Reassuring!

The nurse worked in a practice that specialized in laser eye surgery. Because the surgery was carried out with the patients fully conscious it was a part of her job to keep the patients calm.

Sitting by an especially nervous patient, she could see the perspiration running down his face.

As the doctor finished on one side and moved to the other she wanted to reassure the patient they were halfway to completing a successful procedure.

"There," she said, squeezing his hand. "Now there's only one eye left."

Hisss-terical

Jake staggered back into camp, all battered and bleeding with twigs sticking out of his hair.

"What happened to you?" Joe asked.

"I was chased by a black snake!"

"Silly!" Joe laughed. "Black snakes aren't dangerous."

"They are when they chase you off a cliff!" Jake replied.

Maybe It's Canadian

A man walked into a bar and asked for an ice-cold Less.

The barman shook his head.

"Afraid I don't know that one, sir. Is it one of those foreign beers? An exotic liqueur, perhaps?"

"Beats me," said the man. "I was hoping you recognized it. All I know is the doc said the only way to cure my problems was to drink Less."

Too Good for Your Own Good

A famous doctor was being interviewed by the press. Looking to spice things up a little, one reporter asked if the doctor had ever made any serious mistakes.

"Well, yes," he sighed. "I once cured a billionaire."

"How was that a mistake?" the reporter asked.

The doctor shook his head wearily. "I did it in one visit!"

Because the Doctor Said So

Bud asked Chuck how he broke his arm.

"I had a stomach upset," Chuck replied.

"A stomach upset broke your arm?"

"Don't be so dumb," Chuck said.

"Well, what then?"

"Well, the doc gave me a prescription. 'No matter what,' he said, 'be sure and follow that prescription.' I took it home before I could get it filled and sat it on the table. Then a gust of wind blew it out the window."

"And?"

"Well, I live two floors up. . . ."

His Bite Is Worse than His Bark

A very hardheaded businessman in a very cutthroat industry went to the doctor with a mystery illness. The doctor examined him, checked the results, and rapidly backed away.

"It looks like you have rabies," the sweating doctor said. "It's highly contagious and is nearly always fatal."

The businessman thought for a moment and then asked for a pen and paper.

"A–a–a–are you writing your l–l–last will and testament?" the doctor stammered.

"No," the businessman said. "I'm drawing up a list of people I want to bite!"

"Most surgeons sew, but knitting relaxes me."

3
MD Does Not Stand for "Minor Deity"!

Doctors are highly educated people, and they can do some truly amazing things. Our lives are often in their hands, and their work can seem miraculous at times. It's understandable that nonmedical folk occasionally stand in awe!

Doctors are respected in a way few professions are, but even the most highly trained and skillful of them are simply maintaining, repairing, and caring for a system that's largely beyond their comprehension, a system created by someone altogether smarter. The best of doctors, the humblest of them, know this. . .but some forget.

To the latter group we cheerfully dedicate the following.

Orders From on High

What's the difference between a nurse and a nun?

A nun only serves one God.

A House Call like No Other

A world-famous doctor dies and makes his way to heaven. Arriving at the pearly gates he is not in the best of moods. Finding there's a long line of people waiting to get in, he walks straight to the front.

"That's not the way it works," says Saint Peter. "You have to wait your turn like everyone else."

"But I'm not like everyone else," the doctor insists. "The rich and the famous come to me with their problems. I treat heads of state. The president has my home number in case he needs a house call."

"Sorry," says Saint Peter. "Back of the line. No exceptions."

At that moment a harassed little man rushes by. He carries a doctor's bag, has a stethoscope hanging round his neck, and has a prescription pad in his top pocket.

Without a word Saint Peter opens the gate and lets him in.

"You said no exceptions!" the first doctor yells. "You send possibly the most famous doctor in the world to the back of the line, and then you let an ordinary, insignificant little GP in first!"

"Sorry," says Saint Peter, "but that wasn't a GP. . . . That was God. Sometimes he likes to play at being a doctor."

"Tee, Doctor?"

One elderly man was complaining to another about how difficult it was to get a doctor to make house calls these days.

"Oh I have that all figured out," the other man said. "If I take ill I can usually get a doctor to visit the house within twenty minutes."

"Wow!" The first man was amazed. "How do you manage that?"

"Easy," the second man said. "I bought a house on a golf course!"

Big Shot Doctor

A new nurse listened while the doctor walked about yelling, "Typhoid! Tetanus! Measles!"

She asked a nurse who had been there longer, "Why is he doing that?"

The other nurse replied, "Oh, he just likes to call the shots around here."

Private Consultations

A doctor's girlfriend ended their relationship.

The next day, he billed her for 124 house calls.

No Wonder She Left!

The doctor snapped his fingers at a passing nurse. "Quick," he said, "my secretary has left, and I can't get this to work." He had a handful of documents that he was trying to feed into a machine by his secretary's desk. He jabbed at the start button impatiently but nothing happened.

Despite being busy herself the nurse came over. Spotting the problem, she plugged the shredder in for him.

The doctor, obviously too important to hang around, walked off. As he left the room he shouted back, "I'll need ten copies of those on my desk by tomorrow morning!"

He's Got a Gun—Duck!

A group of doctors decided to treat themselves to a day of duck hunting.

When the first bird appeared in the sky the general practitioner raised his shotgun—and hesitated.

"I think it's a duck," he considered. "But I might need a second opinion on that."

That lucky duck escaped, but another one appeared minutes later. This time the pediatrician noticed it first. He lifted his shotgun—and hesitated. "It might be a duck," he said, "and if it is it might have ducklings. I think I will need to investigate further." And the duck flew away.

Then the psychiatrist spotted a bird. He shouldered his shotgun—and hesitated. "I know it's a duck," he said, "but does *it* know it's a duck?" While he considered the conundrum the duck made good its escape.

Another bird took to the sky. The surgeon whipped his shotgun up. *Boom!*

As the bird dropped to the ground the surgeon turned casually to the pathologist and said, "Go see if that's a duck, will you?"

Lightbulb Transplant

Q. How many surgeons does it take to screw in a lightbulb?

A. Only one. He just holds it up to the socket—and the whole world revolves around him!

Dead on Departure

A frantic nurse ran into the doctor's office. "That man you just gave a clean bill of health to has dropped dead just outside the hospital door. What are we going to do?"

"Quick!" the doctor told the nurse. "Turn him around so it looks as if he was coming in and just didn't get here in time!"

That *Is* Good News!

The doctor called his patient into the office to discuss his test results. "I have some bad news," the doctor said, rising from his desk and walking to the window. "And I have some good news."

He stood looking out the window, and, of course, the patient thought it must be pretty bad if the doctor couldn't face him.

"Give it to me straight, Doc," he said. "What's the bad news?"

"Ohhhh. . .your test results came back. And I doubt you'll last the week."

"That's terrible!" the patient wailed. "How can there be any good news after that?"

"Come here," the doctor said, calmly.

The patient walked over to the doctor, who put a reassuring arm around his shoulder. With his other hand the doctor pointed out to the parking lot.

"The good news is I just got a fantastic deal on that red Ferrari down there!"

An Accidental Miracle

An elderly man is rushed into the hospital and straight into the operating room. Afterward the surgeon tells the nurse that it truly was a close thing. The man had been on the brink of death, but the surgeon's skills saved him.

"One more thing," he said. "I always like my patients to be up on their feet as soon after the operation as possible. It helps prevent blood clots, you know."

Well, the nurse tried her best. After the first few attempts she went to tell the surgeon it just wasn't going to work. The surgeon didn't want to hear it. He insisted she carry out his instructions.

So, day after day, despite the old man's

protestations the nurse got him onto his feet. On the day his family came to collect him he was walking down the corridor to meet them.

They shook the surgeon's hand effusively and told him he was a miracle worker.

"Well. . ." the surgeon tried to appear modest. "I am the best in my field, but miracle worker. . ."

"No, you don't understand," the man's son said. "Dad hadn't walked for a year before he took ill!"

How the Doctor Would Like You to Behave

- Don't expect your doctors to "feel your pain." This would cause them to lose their objectivity.
- Always be cheerful. Your doctor will be having a stressful enough day without you bringing him down.
- Please do try to be suffering from the disease he is treating you for.
- If his treatment does not bring you any relief it's because he has a far deeper understanding of the disease in which your comfort might be incidental or even irrelevant.
- Submitting to experimental clinical

processes will help him and the medical profession immeasurably. Please don't put your self-interest ahead of the greater good.

- Please do not suffer from any ailments your insurance does not cover. That's just getting uppity!

- If the doctor fails to cure you, or even makes your condition worse, remember the patient-doctor relationship is a privileged one, and you have a sacred duty to protect him from exposure.

- Never die while in your doctor's presence or under his direct care. This will be seen as deliberately causing him needless inconvenience and embarrassment.

And the Bibliography, Too!

A man returned his books to the medical library. As he turned to leave the librarian called after him, "Excuse me! But several pages have been removed from the ends of these books!"

"My dear lady," he replied, in his most condescending voice. "You obviously don't know I'm a surgeon. And that's what we do. When we see an appendix—we cut it out!"

A Painful Way to Learn

"You think you've got it hard," an unsympathetic doctor tells his suffering patient. "Why, when I was a student I had angina pectoris and then arteriosclerosis. Just as I was getting over them, I got tuberculosis, pneumonia, and phthisis. Appendicitis was followed by a tonsillectomy. These gave way to aphasia and hypertrophic cirrhosis. I'm not sure how reliable my memory was at that point, but I know I had diabetes, gastritis, rheumatism, lumbago, *and* neuritis!"

The patient was suitably amazed. "How did you get through all that?"

"I really don't know." The doctor shook his head in wonder. "It was the hardest spelling test I've ever had!"

Any More Dumb Questions?

The doctor who performed the autopsy was being cross-examined in a murder case. The rookie lawyer wanted to know if he had checked the victim's pulse before pronouncing him dead.

"No," the doctor said. "I did not check his pulse."

"Did you listen for a heartbeat?" asked the lawyer.

"No I did not," the doctor said.

"So," said the lawyer, "when you signed the

death certificate, you had not really taken any steps to make sure he was dead."

The doctor said, "Well, let me put it this way. The man's brain was in a jar on my desk, but you're right in a way. For all I know he might still have been alive enough to practice law."

Take Another Holiday, Doc, Please!

A surgeon had been on a hunting safari in Africa. After he arrived back at the hospital, a colleague asked him about his holiday.

"Oh, it was a waste of time," the disgusted surgeon said. "I was out there all day every day, and I didn't kill a thing. I would have been better off staying at the hospital!"

The Patient Was "Flushed"

The doctor's wife was always complaining he didn't spend enough time with her, so she arranged a romantic evening in and let him know he'd better be there.

He dutifully turned up and, under her instruction, turned off his pager.

Halfway through the evening the phone rang. Three of his colleagues from the hospital were getting together for a poker night.

"What's that?" he said, loud enough

for his wife to hear. "You need me to come immediately?"

"Is it serious, darling?" his wife asked.

"I'd say so," the doctor replied, straight-faced. "There are three doctors there already!"

Very Precise Surgery

The surgeon removed his mask as he left the operating room.

"Wow!" he said. "That was close!"

"What do you mean?" the surgery nurse asked.

"An inch or two either way," the surgeon said, "and I would have been out of my speciality!"

Charitable Insurance

A Caribbean storm trashed a doctor's multimillion-dollar yacht. The doctor and his steward were washed up on a sandbar with two palm trees, in the middle of nowhere.

The steward was distraught and convinced they would never be found. The doctor, however, was remarkably calm.

"Why aren't you worried, Doc?" the steward asked.

"Well, it's like this," the doctor explained patiently. "Four years ago I gave United Way

$500,000. I gave the same to the United Jewish Appeal. The next year I gave them both $750,000. Business was so good the next year I gave them a million each."

The steward didn't get the connection.

"This is their fund-raising week," the doctor said. "Wanna bet they find me?"

"An aspirin a day will help prevent a heart attack if you have it for lunch instead of a cheeseburger."

4
At the Heart of It All

We abuse it, ignore it, neglect it, but without it where would we be? No wonder some folk say they feel God in their heart. He must feel He has a lot in common with our most vital organ!

Surgeons can tell you in great detail how the heart works; electricity builds up here, it shocks one part of the heart before shocking the other, etcetera. What they can't tell you is why any of that happens. And we're not going to either, because it's too obvious. Instead we're going to have a laugh at our relationship with our primary pump!

Put Your Heart and Soul into This One

Q. What is the difference between God and a cardiologist?

A. The cardiologist might think he's God, but God would never be conceited enough to think he was a cardiologist.

The Information May Have Been Patchy

A patient came in for a routine follow-up appointment with his cardiologist. The doctor asked him how he was doing, and he admitted he was having problems with one of his medications. The doctor asked which med, and the patient said it was the patch. He'd read the instructions carefully and followed them to the letter. The instruction said to apply a new patch every six hours.

"So, what's the problem?" the doctor asked.

"Well," the patient replied a little sheepishly, "I'm running out of places to put them."

The doctor had him undress, and, sure enough, the patient had patches all over his body.

Now the patches come in a new box that

has the instruction in bold red letters, "Remove old patch before applying a new one."

Hear What You Want to Hear

A ninety-two-year-old man went to the doctor to get a physical. A few days later the doctor was driving along the street when he saw his elderly patient walking along with a gorgeous young lady on his arm.

The next time the man came into the office the doctor congratulated him on his new companion. "Well," the old fellow grinned, "I got you to thank for it, Doc!"

"How do you figure?" the doctor asked.

"Just doing what you said Doc—'Get a hot mama, and be cheerful.'"

The doctor spluttered, "I didn't say that! I said you've got a heart murmur. Be careful!"

Put Some Grease on That Left Ventricle

The car was up on the lift, and the mechanic was working on the engine. He'd seen the car's owner and thought he looked familiar. The owner was filling out some paperwork when the mechanic realized he was one of the country's most famous cardiac surgeons. The mechanic had seen him on the news countless times.

Determined to bring the big shot down a peg or two he shouted the owner over to where he was working.

Puffing out his chest and raising his voice so all the guys could hear him, the mechanic said, "Check this, Mr. Fancy-pants Cardiologist. You ain't the only one that fixes hearts. This here engine is the heart of your car. I'll take the valves out, grind them, put them back in, or completely replace them. When I'm done this old sweetheart of yours is gonna run like a teenager! Anything you can do, Doc, I can do!"

Surprised, the cardiologist nodded. "Sure," he said. He thought for a moment, then added, "Let's see you do it with the engine running!"

Try Getting Blood from That!

A passing policeman spotted a man in a white coat searching through the bushes outside a hospital.

"Lost something, Doc?"

"Nuh-uh," the doctor replied. "We're gonna be doing a heart transplant on a tax inspector later. Just trying to find a stone the right size."

Stop Bleating about Your Health Problems!

A man needed a heart transplant, but there were no human organs available. Things were getting desperate, so the surgeon suggested the possibility of using a sheep's heart. Deciding he really had no choice, the man signed the consent form.

The operation went well, and the next day the surgeon came to see the patient.

"And how are you feeling?" he asked.

The man replied, "Oh, you know. Not baaaaaad."

Don't Let His Heart Rule Your Head

A man had a heart attack and was rushed into the hospital. It was decided his heart was failing completely. He needed a transplant!

"You're in luck!" the doctor told him. "We have two hearts available, so you get to choose. One of them belonged to an attorney; the other belonged to a social worker. Which one do you want?"

Straightaway the man said, "The attorney's!"

"Wow, what made you choose that one?" the doctor asked.

"Well," the man explained, "everyone knows social workers have good hearts, but they can sometimes be bleeding hearts. The attorney's, on the other hand, has probably never been used, so it'll be as good as new!"

Family Connections

A man was traveling in Italy when he had a heart attack. He was rushed to the nearest hospital, where they performed a quadruple bypass.

When he woke up he found he was being cared for by nuns. They gently broke it to him that the bill for such a complex operation would be substantial.

He decided he wasn't going to pay it. What could they do, take the heart back?

The nun asked him if he had health insurance.

"Nope," he replied. "No insurance."

"Do you have any savings?" she asked. He shook his head.

"Well, do you have any relatives who might help you pay the bill?" the nun asked.

Getting a little tired of this, the man snapped, "I only have a spinster sister. She's a nun, too!"

Now it was the nun's turn to be annoyed. "Nuns are not spinsters!" she insisted. "They are married to God!"

"In that case," the man retorted, "I do

have family who can help. Send the bill to my brother-in-law!"

Talk about Healthy!

The Japanese diet is low in fat, and their rate of heart disease is lower than that in the United States, the United Kingdom, and Australia.

But the French diet is high in fat, and their rate of heart disease is lower than that in the United States, the United Kingdom, and Australia.

The intake of red wine in India is low, and their rate of heart disease is lower than that in the United States, the United Kingdom, and Australia.

But the intake of red wine in Spain is high, and their rate of heart disease is lower than that in the United States, the United Kingdom, and Australia.

So what conclusion do we draw from this? Eat and drink as much as you like. It's speaking English that is bad for you!

That's a Relief!

Joe arrives home after an operation to fit a pacemaker to his heart.

Once all the well-wishers have left Joe

settles down. With nothing else to do he reads the instructions that came with the pacemaker.

At one point it said the unit comes with a lifetime guarantee.

"Cool," Joe says to himself. "That'll save me worrying about how to change the battery."

Don't Have a Heart Attack, But. . .

While Joe was in the hospital having a heart bypass operation, his friends heard he had won a hundred million dollars in a lottery. No one wanted to tell him the news. They were all convinced the shock would cause him to fall down dead.

Eventually the family doctor was appointed to tell him.

Trying to be diplomatic, the doctor said, "Say, Joe, supposing you were to win a hundred million dollars. What do you reckon you would do with it?"

Joe considered it. "Well, Doc," he said. "I ain't got no kids, and I already have everything I need. You've always looked after me fine. So, I think I'd give half to you."

And the doctor fell down dead!

I'd Like to Donate Everything but My Blood, My Organs, My Body, My Money, My Car...

Bubba always carried a donor card wherever he went. If he got run over by a truck he wanted someone else to get the use of that card!

The Devil's Die-t Plan

In the beginning God created a world full of green vegetables so man and woman would have long lives. Satan created the fast-food joint and asked man, "Do you want fries with that?"

God created healthy yogurts so woman might keep the figure man found so desirable. And Satan created chocolate. Man and woman piled on the pounds!

God showed man and woman how to cook with olive oil to keep their cholesterol down. Satan invented ice cream and chocolate chip cookies.

God invented running shoes and cool training gear to help man and woman get fit. Satan invented satellite television and the remote control.

God invented the potato, a low-fat food that was high in nutrition. Satan sliced it, deep-fried it, and created many dips to go with it.

Man and woman ate chips in front of the

TV because they were too large to do anything else. Satan saw it and said, "It is good."

Man went into cardiac arrest. God sighed and created heart-transplant surgery.

Satan grinned and created HMOs.

Not *That* Much of an Emergency

A husband and wife were playing on the ninth green when she collapsed from a heart attack.

"Help me, darling!" she gasped.

Her husband ran to get some help. A little while later he came back, picked up his club, and began to line up his shot on the green. His wife lifted her head and wheezed, "I may be dying—and you're putting?"

"Don't worry, honey," he said. "I found a cardiologist on the second hole who said he would come and help."

"Why didn't he come back with you?" she whispered.

"He'll be here soon," the husband said, practicing his putt. "Everyone else has already agreed to let him play through."

Rescue Me from High School Kids

High school students were practicing cardiac compressions on the mannequin known as

Rescue Anne or Resusci-Annie. Just a limbless plastic torso and head with inflatable lungs and a pressure pad for a heart, Annie is the perfect CPR patient.

It was the class comedian's turn to revive Annie, but before he started pumping on her plastic heart he opened her mouth and cleared her airways. Then he put his cheek to her mouth to feel if she was breathing.

"What's that, Annie!" He sat up, seemingly startled, and turned to his teacher. "She says she can't feel her legs!"

No Trouble at All

Helen accompanied her aunt Sarah to the cardiologist's. First he wanted to take down some details, so he asked if there was a history of heart trouble in the family.

Sarah shook her head. "No, I don't think so. Why? What do you mean?"

The doctor asked the rest of his questions and then left the room.

"Aunt Sarah," Helen whispered, "weren't you being a little, well. . .free with the truth there?"

"What do you mean dear?" Aunt Sarah asked.

"Well," Helen went on quietly, "didn't your

dad, your aunt, your brother, and your grandma all have heart attacks?"

"Yes, dear," Aunt Sarah replied. "But they just had heart attacks and they died. It wasn't any trouble."

"It's a new medical technology. Instead of crying, we can program your choice of 200 fun ring tones!"

5
In the Beginning. . .

There's a story of a four-year-old leaning over her newborn baby brother's crib. The mom and dad, afraid she might be jealous of the new family member, listen in. "Tell me what God's like," they hear their daughter whisper, "because I'm beginning to forget." Corny (and not a little heart tugging) as that story may be, it has more than a grain of truth in it. We are very near God as we welcome children into this world. They, in turn, remember God's heart well enough not to take this world too seriously. . .so we won't either!

Good Baby, Baaaaad Mommy!

A three-year-old boy was getting bored in the doctor's waiting room. Looking around he spotted a heavily pregnant lady. He wandered over and, with all the innocence of childhood, asked, "Why is your stomach so big?"

She smiled and replied, "Because I have a baby in there."

The boy's eyes widened like saucers. "There's a baby in your stomach?"

"There sure is," she replied.

The boy considered this news for a moment with a real puzzled expression, and then he asked, "Is it a good baby?"

"Oh yes," she replied. "It's a very good baby."

The boy shook his head with disbelief.

"Then why did you eat him?"

Just Don't Add Jalapeños

The public-health nurse was teaching new parents some of the little things involved in caring for a new baby.

As she was demonstrating how to wrap a newborn, a young Asian couple turned to her and said, "You mean we should wrap the baby like an egg roll?"

"Yes," she replied. "That's exactly right." It was such a good analogy she kept using it until one anxious mother said, "I don't know how to make egg rolls. Can I wrap my baby like a burrito?"

Baby, Beta

The midwife was showing the soon-to-be-mom around the delivery suite. "Things have really changed since the old days," she said. "Now we have all the latest high-tech, infrared, ultrasonic, remotely controlled equipment."

"Wow," said the easily impressed young woman. "So, is there any chance when the baby's born that it might actually be cordless?"

Well. . .Duh!

A man speaks frantically into the phone, "My wife is pregnant, and her contractions are only two minutes apart!"

"Is this her first child?" the doctor queries.

"No, you idiot!" the man shouts. "This is her husband!"

That's Stating the Obvious

The nurse came into the waiting room and told the anxious man he was a daddy. Mother and all the babies were doing well.

"All the babies?" he exclaimed.

"That's right." she said. "You're the father of quintuplets!"

She took the stunned man through to the nursery to see his children. He reached out to pick one of the babies up—but the nurse stopped him.

"You can't. You're not sterile."

The man looked down at his five new babies.

"You're telling me!"

Crazy Craving

Did you hear about the pregnant woman who had a craving for eating rubber?

She had a bouncing baby boy!

The Big Momma

They say that somewhere in the world a woman gives birth every minute.

Someone should really find that woman and find out how she's doing that!

How to Tell the Difference

Two newly born babies lay in their cribs in the maternity ward. In baby language one asked the other, "Are you a boy baby or a girl baby?"

The other one said, "Oh, I'm a boy baby!"

The first one said, "How can you be so sure?"

"Easy," the boy baby said. He kicked off his blanket, wriggled up his nightie, and said, "Look. . .blue booties!"

Around Here Somewhere

A seventy-year-old woman was determined to become a mom, and eventually, with the help of a lot of fertility experts and expensive treatments, her wish came true.

Her shocked but delighted family and friends came to the hospital all excited to see the baby. After they had talked to mom for a while they asked to see the baby.

"Oh, later," she said.

So they talked some more and then asked again.

"Later, later," she said.

Eventually the visitors were running out of small talk and asked when they could see the baby.

"You can see it when it cries," the mom said.

"But why do we have to wait until it cries?" they asked.

"Ohh," the mom sighed, "because I can't remember where I put it!"

Thank Goodness It Wasn't a Fortune 500

The nurse came into the maternity ward waiting room and told a nervous father-to-be he could relax; he was now the father of healthy twins. After he finished whooping and hollering he winked at the other guys and said, "That's because I work for the Doublemint Company!"

Shortly afterward the nurse told one of the other men his wife just gave birth to triplets. "You are kidding!" he said. He turned to the third guy and said, "That's amazing! I work for the 3M Company."

Ten minutes later the nurse found the third guy outside, pacing up and down frantically. "There's nothing to worry about," she said. "Your wife's doing fine."

"No, you don't understand," he said. "You saw what happened with other guys. Well, I work for 7-Up!"

Feeling No Pain

An experienced mom was preparing a birthing plan with her midwife.

"And what about pain relief?" the midwife asked. "Are you going to go natural?"

"Oh no," the mom said. "I want an epidural."

"At what point?" said the midwife, taking notes.

The mom replied, "Some time in the eighth month would be just fine!"

We Three Docs of Orient Are

A mother and daughter turn up at the doctor's office with some worrying symptoms. It takes the doctor only a few minutes to determine that the girl is pregnant. The girl looks embarrassed, but the mother indignantly refuses to accept the possibility.

The doctor insists she is—the mother insists that's impossible.

Recognizing a lost cause when he sees one, the doctor walks over to the window and stares, intently, out toward the horizon.

"Why aren't you doing anything?" the mother asks.

"Oh, but I am," the doctor says. "The last time this happened a star appeared in the east, and three wise men showed up. I'm hoping they can help me figure out what's causing your daughter's symptoms."

Maybe We Could Come to an Arrangement

A child psychologist was addressing a class of parents-to-be, many of whom already had at least one child. Tackling the issue of breaking the big news to the children, he said, "Some parents tell the children, 'Having you was so much fun we decided to get another child.' But, think about it, ladies. Imagine your husband said, 'Honey, I love having you as a wife so much I decided to bring home another wife.' What would you say?"

One of the older mothers piped up immediately. "Does she cook?"

Bubba's Babies

Bubba's wife was having their first baby. When the doctor got to the tin shack in the backwoods he found there was no electricity, and it was starting to get dark.

Bubba offered to light the lamp and hold it so the doctor could see.

Eventually the baby arrived, and Bubba was delighted.

"Hold that light steady," the doctor said. "There's another one coming!"

A stunned Bubba leaned closer. His second child came into the world.

"There's another one coming!" the doctor said.

A totally shell-shocked Bubba looked from his wife to the lamp to the doctor and said, "Hey, doc, do you think it's the light that's attracting them?"

That Sinking—and Swelling—Feeling

A man asks a pretty young woman to dance. He asks what she does, and she tells him she is a nurse. Feeling flushed with excitement, he whispers in her ear, "I wish I could catch something and let you treat me."

"That would really be something," she whispers back.

"Would it?" he says, grinning.

"It sure would," she replies. "I work in the maternity ward. You'd have to catch pregnancy."

Don't Throw It Back, This One's a Keeper

A prenatal group was being shown around the maternity ward of a hospital. The moms- and dads-to-be had just arrived at the nursery when a newborn baby was brought in.

Excitedly, all the moms tried to guess the weight. Some were close, but the nurse said no one was spot on. Smiling, she turned to the dads and held the baby up. "Any of you gentlemen care to guess?"

The guys nervously blushed and backed away—except for one man.

"Eight pounds three," he said.

"Why, that's absolutely right," the nurse said. "How did you know?"

The man shrugged. "I'm a fisherman."

Enough Is Enough

A man had just completed his annual physical.

"You're in good shape but a little run-down. Is there anything you want to ask me about?"

"Well, doc," the man said wearily, "I'm thinking of having a vasectomy."

"Well," said the doctor, "that's a serious decision. What does your family think?"

"Oh, they're for it!" the man said. "Twenty-two to three!

"What fits your busy schedule better, exercising 30 minutes a day or being dead 24 hours a day?"

6
. . . And Out the End

In general death is an undignified, inglorious thing. It completely disregards our plans and takes us when it feels like it. So. . .what are we going to do? Give in to despair? Wail that there is no point to any of it? Or, knowing that there's more ahead after this life, do we laugh at it all and tell death to. . .well. . .get a life?

Hopefully, this next section will help make that decision easier. Or, at the very least it will give you a chuckle while you are making up your mind!

Death, where is thy sting? Joke, where is thy punch line?

A Short but Successful Career

The artist's painting had been on display for a week when he asked the gallery owner if there had been any interest in his work.

"Well, I have good news and bad news," the owner replied. "The good news is that a wealthy-looking gentleman did ask about your work. He was wondering if it would appreciate in value after your death. When I told him I was pretty sure it would, he bought all your paintings."

"But that's fantastic!" the artist yelled. "And what's the bad news?"

The gallery owner swallowed hard.

"I think he was your doctor."

How to Break the Bad News

A group of married men got together to play some poker. Kenny was losing badly and then his luck got even worse. He grabbed his chest and fell out of his chair. One of the guys was a doctor, and he pronounced Kenny dead of a heart attack.

No one knew how they were going to tell his wife about this, but the doctor was used to telling people bad news, so he offered to do it. "You have to tell the truth, but make it seem like a good thing."

Shortly afterward he rang the bell at Kenny's house. His wife answered, and the doctor said, "I have to tell you, Kenny was gambling with us, and he just lost $5,000."

Kenny's wife flipped. "That money was for our holiday! Well you can tell Kenny from me he should just drop dead!"

"Well, okay," the doctor said. "If you're sure. . ."

You Got Here Just in Time

Pete hasn't been feeling too good, so he goes to his doctor for a complete checkup.

Afterward the doctor comes out with the results. "I'm afraid I have some very bad news," the doctor says. "You're dying, and you don't have much time left."

"Oh, that's terrible!" says Pete. "How long have I got?"

"Ten," the doctor says sadly.

"Ten?" Pete asks, confused. "Ten what? Years? Months? Weeks? What?"

"Nine. . ."

Too Much Love Will Kill You

A woman accompanied her husband to the doctor's office. After his checkup the doctor asked him to take a seat in the waiting room. He asked the woman to come into his office.

"Your husband is suffering from heart problems, and his stress levels are through the roof," he said. "If you don't do the following, your husband will surely die.

"Each morning, fix him a healthy breakfast. Be pleasant, and make sure he is in a good mood. For lunch make him a fresh, nutritious meal. For dinner prepare an especially nice meal for him.

"Don't burden him with chores, as he probably had a hard day. Don't discuss your problems with him; it will only make his stress worse. And most importantly, make love with your husband several times a week and satisfy his every whim. If you can do this for the next ten months to a year, I think your husband will regain his health completely."

On the way home, the husband asked his

wife, "What did the doctor say?"

She thought about it for a moment and then said, "You're going to die."

The Cheek of It!

The doctor may *tell* you you're going to be okay, but when they give you one of those skimpy gowns with laces at the back you just know your end is in sight!

Daft Definition of Death

You won't find it in any medical dictionary, but for most medics the perfect definition of "death" is: Just how far some patients will go to make things awkward for their doctor!

Final Demand—Final Reply

The owner of a small business called his friend and said, "Promise me that when I die you will make sure I'm cremated!"

"Okay," his surprised friend said. "And what should I do with the ashes?"

"Oh," the businessman replied, "just send them to the IRS with a note saying, 'Now you've got everything!'"

Mmm?

"I'm worried about your heart murmur," the doc told Jack.

"I've always had a heart murmur," Jack protested.

"Yeah," replied the doc, "but now the murmur has started humming."

"That doesn't sound good!" Jack was getting worried now.

"It's worse than you think," the doc said. "It's humming 'Nearer My God to Thee'!"

Old **Buddies**

Walter was looking forward to attending his fiftieth class reunion, but when he got there his surviving classmates only seemed to want to talk about all their ailments. This one had heart problems, another one had kidney stones, someone else was waiting for a liver transplant.

When he got back home his wife asked how it went. "Oh, it wasn't much like a reunion," Walter sighed. "It was more of an organ recital."

Exercise Is Bad for You

A woman went to the doctor on behalf of her elderly husband. The doctor gave her a course of pills.

"Have him take two of these on Monday, Wednesday, and Fridays," the doctor said. "Just skip the other days."

A month later the woman comes in to tell the doctor her husband had died. The doctor was stunned.

"Surely not," he gasped. "Was it a side effect of the pills?"

"No," she said. "It was all the skipping that killed him."

Non-Habit-Forming Medication

Ralph looked really upset when he got back from seeing the doctor.

"What's up, honey?" his wife asked.

"It's terrible!" Ralph cried. "Awful! The doc told me I'm going to have to take a pill every day for the rest of my life!"

"Well. . .that's not so bad, is it?"

"Not so bad? Not so bad? I opened the packet in the car. There are five pills in it!"

Today's My Lucky Day—But Tomorrow Doesn't Look So Good

Wayne had been feeling really awful, so he went for a checkup.

"It's bad news," the doc told him. "You

have a disease called Yellow 24. It's called that because eventually your internal organs turn yellow, and you then have twenty-four hours to live. I'd say your organs just changed color."

Devastated, he told his wife. She was sympathetic, but she didn't want this to ruin her regular night out at bingo, so she insisted he come along, too.

Deciding to play to take his mind off his impending death, Wayne got one line and won a hundred bucks. Twenty minutes later he got another and won two hundred bucks. He won the next game—and the next—and the next!

Eventually the bingo caller got him up on the stage. "This is your first time at bingo, and you've won nine hundred dollars! You must be the luckiest man alive!"

"Well. . .no, not really," Wayne spoke shyly into the microphone. "You see. . .I've got Yellow 24."

The bingo caller picked up a piece of paper from his console.

"I don't believe it," he shouted. "Ladies and gentlemen, he's won the raffle as well!"

Well, That's a Relief

Bob just couldn't seem to get the chirpy receptionist to understand how urgently he needed to see the doctor.

"Would 10:30 next week on Tuesday be good for you?" she asked breezily.

"That's eleven days away," he spluttered. "I could be dead by then!"

"Oh don't worry about that," the receptionist reassured Bob. "If your wife calls us on Monday morning we can cancel the appointment."

Five Minutes

There was a sign on the wall of the hospital delivery room that said, "The first five minutes of someone's life are the most critical."

Under that someone had scribbled, "The last five are pretty risky, too!"

Too Young to Die

After a long and serious operation a woman slipped into a coma. The doctors did everything they could, but eventually they had to admit defeat. They called the husband into the room to ask his permission to turn the life support off.

The husband was understandably distraught.

"But, Doctor!" he wailed. "It's so unfair. She's too young to die. She's only forty-five!"

His wife sat up like a shot.

"Shut up!" she squealed. "I'm only thirty-eight!"

Being Dead Doesn't Mean You Can't Still Travel

A mortuary technician was transporting a body through the hospital when his gurney hit a folder someone had dropped. The technician fell, and the coffin slid off the gurney. It bumped through a door and slid down the stairs, picking up momentum as it went. It crashed though the doors on the floor below and went sliding along the polished floor, scaring the wits out of several patients and staff.

But a quick-thinking pharmacist grabbed a bottle of cough medicine. As the wooden box skidded past him the pharmacist poured the syrup over it from one end to the other—and the coffin stopped!

An Extended Stay

A patient was understandably upset when the doctor told him he had only six months to live.

"So," said the doctor trying to distract the patient with some small talk, "how do you think you'll spend your last six months?"

The patient did some frantic thinking.

"Well, I reckon I'll invite my wife's mother to stay, I'll give up drinking, and I'll start doing all those chores around the house I've been avoiding since we moved in there."

"Really?" said the surprised doctor. "Why?"

"Because," said the patient. "That way it'll be the longest six months of my life!"

Clean Hands Save Lives

"I use so much alcohol-based hand sanitizer, my hands had to join a 12-step program!"

7
Angels on Overtime

Most nurses don't like being called "angels." It implies an otherworldly calling and somehow removes them from expectations of decent pay and working conditions. But the nickname sticks, and that surely reflects the admiration society has for them.

And the fact that they aren't otherworldly beings but overworked, harassed human beings (often with a wicked sense of humor) is a wonderful thing in itself.

When it comes to loving one another the way Jesus said, we do our best. But until we get better at it we will have those "angels" we call nurses to show us how it's done.

Ticket Tape

A highway patrol officer was rushed into the hospital with an inflamed appendix. The doctors operated and everything went well. But lying in bed afterward, the officer felt sharp pains across his chest every time he moved. Panicking that something else might have gone wrong he gingerly lifted his hospital gown.

Taped firmly across his hairy chest were three wide strips of adhesive tape, the kind that doesn't come off easily. Written in large black letters were the words: "Get well soon! From the nurse you gave a ticket to last week."

Tennis Elbow

A surgeon stops a nurse to brief her on a patient's condition. He's particularly concerned that this fellow gets the best attention.

"The patient is a doctor," he tells the nurse, "but more importantly he's my favorite tennis partner. His surgery was really quite intricate, and I'm worried it's going to affect his game. To make sure he gets his full use of his tennis arm I want you to give him injections in the specified points every twenty minutes, with a backup injection five minutes after each of the first lot.

"He'll need these pills on the hour every hour, these pills every eighty minutes, and four of these pills four times a day. Despite all those pills he needs to drink no more than ten ounces of water every half hour, and he must visit the toilet immediately after each drink.

"His arm needs to be soaked in ice water for ten minutes followed by ten minutes in warm water, followed by ten minutes in lukewarm water, and this is to be repeated all day. Only take his arm out of the water for light physiotherapy every hundred minutes.

"Back rubs and foot massages should be ongoing, and, above all, maintain a cheerful reassuring disposition with him at all times."

The nurse lays down the pile of charts for all her other patients and goes to the man's bedside. Recovered from the anesthetic the doctor asks her how the operation went.

"Oh," she said, cheerfully, "the surgeon says

it all went fine. But he says you'll never play tennis again."

You Know You're a Real Nurse If. . . (Part 1)

- you wash your hands for a full minute even in a restaurant washroom—and turn off the taps with your elbows!
- your favorite dream is the one where you leave a mess at a patient's bedside and tell a doctor to clean it up.
- you believe all patients need TLC— Thorazine, Lorazepam, and Compazine.
- everyone, including complete strangers, wants you to look at something they haven't shown anyone else.
- you want to go ballistic on your TV every time you see a nurse on a soap opera with perfectly applied makeup and doing nothing but talking on the phone and flirting with doctors.
- you've told a difficult patient your name was that of your coworker and that they were to holler if they needed help.
- you don't worry too much about blood loss—unless it's your own!
- You can almost see the germs on doorknobs and telephones.

- you find yourself checking out other customers' arm veins in grocery waiting lines.
- you know the phone numbers of every late-night food delivery place in town by heart.

Has the Air-Con Broken?

A nurse died from exhaustion. Thanks to an administrative mix-up in the afterlife she ended up in hell.

It took her three weeks to realize she wasn't still at work!

What a Break!

Two nurses and a supervisor were chatting on their lunch break. Suddenly the room filled with smoke, and a genie appeared.

"Because of your unending kindness," he announced, "I have come to grant you each a wish."

The first nurse wished she was on a tropical island with a hunky native man taking care of her every desire. In a flash and a puff of smoke—she disappeared!

The second nurse wished she was at a lodge in the mountains, where the skiing was good and the après-ski was even better. Flash, puff—and she was gone!

"And you, madam," the genie turned to the supervisor, "what is your heart's greatest desire?"

The supervisor stood up and gave the genie her sternest look. "That those two be back at work the minute their lunch break is finished!"

Let the Chase Commence!

The senior nurse was showing some female nursing students around the hospital. Walking through a ward full of male patients, she turned to the young nurses.

"This, ladies," she said, "is the most hazardous part of the hospital."

"Why?" one confused student asked. "Because they're getting radiation therapy?"

"No," said the senior nurse. "Because they're almost well again!"

Feathers for Breakfast

Checking on a patient in the morning, the nurse discovered he had eaten his pillow during the night.

"How do you feel?" she asked.

"Oh," he sighed, "a little down in the mouth."

A Wicked Sense of Humor

The patient was actually a local gangster and well known to the hospital staff. After his operation he woke to find himself in a dark room.

"Why are all the blinds closed?" he asked the nurse working by his bedside.

"Well," the nurse replied, "they're fighting a huge fire across the street, and we didn't want you to wake up and think the operation had failed."

Not So Reassuring

As part of an investigation the hospital administrator asked the patient, "Would you mind telling me why you ran, screaming, from the operating room?"

"Because I heard the nurse say, 'Don't be afraid. An appendectomy is quite a simple operation.'"

The administrator was confused. "Surely, that would have been a reassuring thing to hear."

"She wasn't talking to me!" the patient yelled. "She was talking to the surgeon!"

Speaking in Tongues

The nurse told the little boy in the waiting

room, "Don't forget to stick your tongue out for the doctor."

"Why?" his mom asked.

"Oh," the nurse replied, "I just don't like him."

That'll Make Her See Red!

A senior nurse asked her colleague why the new student nurse always carried a red marking pen with her wherever she went.

Trying hard to keep a straight face, her colleague said, "Someone told her a big part of the job was drawing blood."

You Know You're a Real Nurse If... (Part 2)

- you would like to meet the inventor of the call light in a dark alley one night.
- you can watch the goriest movie and eat spaghetti with lots of tomato sauce afterward.
- you use a plastic 30cc medicine cup for a shot glass.
- you believe not all patients are annoying ...some are asleep.
- every time you walk, no matter where you are, you rattle with all the scissors and clamps in your pockets.

- you can tell the pharmacist more about the medicines he dispenses than he can.
- you refuse to watch *E.R.* on television in case it triggers flashbacks.
- you live by the motto, "To diagnose correctly is only half the battle, convincing the doctor is the other half."
- you can sleep soundly sitting up at a hospital cafeteria table during dinner break.
- you avoid unhealthy-looking shoppers in the mall for fear that they'll drop near you and you'll have to do CPR on your day off.
- you know when it's a full moon without having to look outside.

Where the Bad Docs Go

A doctor died and found himself outside the pearly gates. Unfortunately he'd been a bad lot when he arrived, and entry into heaven wasn't automatic. Saint Peter met him outside the pearly gates and told him he had to choose which way he would go in the afterlife.

Three doors appeared in front of him. The doctor opened the first and peeked through. It was a nightmare of fire, brimstone, and tortured souls. He slammed the door shut. "Not that way, thanks!"

He opened the second door and found an endless line of lawyers waiting to sue him for all his malpractices during his life.

"Nuh-uh!" He slammed the second door shut.

Behind the third door were lots of doctors and surgeons being waited on hand and foot by beautiful young women in skimpy nurse's outfits.

"Yes, please! I'll go this way!"

A surprised Saint Peter looked around the door and said, "Oops, my mistake. That's nurses' hell."

How to Get a Doctor's Attention

Two senior nurses were complaining about the pretty new nurse who was getting all the attention around the hospital.

"I hear she's going to change her name to A. Pendix," said one nurse.

"Yes," said the other nurse. "Some women will go to any length to get a surgeon to take them out!"

It's Just Like That ("Facts" about Life as a Nurse)

- The doctor only ever asks what your name is when the patient isn't doing well.
- The patient farthest away from the nurses' station will ring the call bell way more often than the patient closest to the nurses' station.
- If you wear a crisp new uniform someone will throw up on it.
- The correct depth for chest compression will be half an inch less than you went when you broke that guy's ribs.
- Your nose will always start to itch just after you scrub up, get gloved and gowned, and go into surgery.
- When management cancels those extra members of staff because it's been so quiet—look out!
- Staff meetings will always be scheduled after you have worked a double shift and just want to get to bed.
- You will walk all the way across the hospital to get to the storeroom—and forget what you came for. Don't worry; you'll remember when you get back to where you started from.
- Your successes will only happen when no

one is looking. Your failures will always occur when the doctor is looking over your shoulder.

- The more expensive the piece of equipment, the more often it will break down.
- Nursing experience is something that usually arrives five minutes after you needed it.
- As soon as you order pizza for delivery, ten drunks and four heart attack patients will turn up at the ER.

Good Luck and Good-bye

There's a certain kind of nurse who can still smile even when everyone else is losing their heads, when the ward is understaffed, when all the monitors are beeping at once, when the doctors are panicking and the patients are complaining.

She's the nurse going home after a sixteen-hour shift!

Things You Say Most Often if You're a Nurse

- "No, nurses only wear *those* uniforms in the movies."

- "No, I will not give you a bed bath!" (To every other guy they meet.)
- "Honestly, you won't feel a thing."
- "Because the doctor said so."
- "I swear, if he rings that call bell one more time. . ."
- "You might feel a little sick."
- "How can I help you?" (A million times a shift.)
- And the one nurses really enjoy saying, "Doctor, I'm sorry to wake you, but. . ."

"Play some Frisbee, chew on an old sock, bark at a squirrel. If that doesn't make you feel better, eat some cheese with a pill in it."

8
Doctor, Doctor. . .

General practitioners are increasingly busy these days, and appointments are nowhere near as long as they used to be. Thankfully, they tend to be a bit longer than these "Doctor, Doctor" jokes!

Doctors do a great job, but if occasionally— very, very occasionally—their diagnoses are a little like some of the replies printed below, it's because of time constraints imposed on them and because the medical profession, for all its huge advances, is only just beginning to really understand how "fearfully and wonderfully" made we really are.

What's that, you say? An embarrassing problem? Come on in and tell the doctor!

Patient: "Doctor, Doctor, I feel like I'm a biscuit!"

Doctor: "What, one of those square ones you put butter and cheese on?"

Patient: "That's right! What does it mean?"

Doctor: "It means you're crackers!"

Patient: "Doctor, Doctor, I've lost my memory!"

Doctor: "When did you lose it?"

Patient: "When did I lose what?"

Patient: "Doctor, Doctor, I feel like a bridge!"

Doctor: "Goodness me. What's come over you?"

Patient: "Two buses, twenty-five cars, a motorbike, and a train."

Patient: "Doctor, Doctor, I keep losing my temper with people."

Doctor: "Sit down and tell me about it."

Patient: "I just did, you stupid quack!"

Patient: "Doctor, Doctor, I feel like a
   needle!"
Doctor: "Yes, I can see your point."

Patient: "Doctor, Doctor, I feel like a pair of
   curtains!"
Doctor: "Oh, pull yourself together man!"

Patient: "Doctor, Doctor, I snore so loudly
   I wake myself up. What can I do?"
Doctor: "Sleep in another room."

Patient: "Doctor, Doctor, I keep hearing a
   ringing noise!"
Doctor: "Well, try answering the phone!"

Patient: "Doctor, Doctor, everyone thinks
   that I am a liar!"
Doctor: "Ohhh, I can't believe that!"

Patient: "Doctor, Doctor, I think that I
   need glasses!"
"Doctor": "I think so too—this is a candy
   store!"

Patient: "Doctor, Doctor, I broke my leg in
   four places!"
Doctor: "Well, don't go back to those
   places!"

Patient: "Doctor, Doctor, I get a pain in my eye whenever I drink juice!"

Doctor: "Try taking the straw out first."

Patient: "Doctor, Doctor, I have the strangest feeling that I'm invisible!"

Doctor: "What? Who said that?"

Patient: "Doctor, Doctor, I swallowed a bone."

Doctor: "Are you choking?"

Patient: "No, I really did!"

Patient: "Doctor, Doctor, I think I'm a bell."

Doctor: "Well, take these pills, and if you don't feel better give me a ring!"

Patient: "Doctor, Doctor, I dream beautiful women come into my bedroom every night."

Doctor: "What do you do then?"

Patient: "I fight them off all night."

Doctor: "And what do you want me to do for you?"

Patient: "Break my arms!"

Patient: "Doctor, Doctor, I think I'm suffering from déjà vu!"

Doctor: "No you're not."

Patient: "How do you know?"

Doctor: "Because you were in here yesterday complaining of the same thing."

Patient: "Doctor, Doctor, I keep thinking I'm a bee!"

Doctor: "Stop bothering me, would you? Buzz off!"

Patient: "Doctor, Doctor, it's these pills you gave me for my body odor. . ."

Doctor: "What about them? Aren't they working?"

Patient: "Well, they might, if they didn't keep slipping out from under my arms!"

Patient: "Doctor, Doctor, I've had a stomachache since I ate a lobster yesterday."

Doctor: "Well, did the meat smell bad when you took it out of the shell?"

Patient: "You're supposed to take it out of the shell?"

Patient: "Doctor, Doctor, I keep dreaming I'm a sheep!"

Doctor: "Oh, dear. That's baaaaaaaaaad!"

Patient: "Doctor, Doctor, sometimes I think I'm a tepee, and then I think I'm a wigwam."

Doctor: "Oh, relax! You're just too tents."

Patient: "Doctor, Doctor, I think I'm a moth!"

Doctor: "That's a psychiatric problem. Why did you come in here?"

Patient: "Well, I saw the light shining through your window. . . ."

Patient: "Doctor, Doctor, I think I'm a vampire!"

Doctor: "Necks, please!"

Patient: "Doctor, Doctor, I think I'm a kleptomaniac."

Doctor: "Don't worry; I have something you can take for that."

Patient: "Doctor, Doctor, I sometimes think I'm a frog!"

Doctor: "Well, that's not too bad."

Patient: "Yeah, but I'm afraid I'm going to croak!"

Patient: "Doctor, Doctor, I feel like I'm a pack of playing cards!"

Doctor: "Sit over there and I'll deal with you later."

Patient: "Doctor, Doctor, have you anything for a really bad headache?"
Doctor: "Bend over and run head first at the wall. That should do it!"

Patient: "Doctor, Doctor, will this ointment clear up my spots?"
Doctor: "I never make rash promises."

Patient: "Doctor, Doctor, I have this compulsion to paint myself gold!"
Doctor: "Don't worry; it's just a gilt complex."

Patient: "Doctor, Doctor, I think I'm slowly becoming invisible!"
Doctor: "Yes, I can see you're not all there."

Patient: "Doctor, Doctor, I'm convinced I'm a yo-yo!"
Doctor: "Ahh, you're just stringing me along!"

Patient: "Doctor, Doctor, you have to help me right now. I'm shrinking!"
Doctor: "Can't you see I'm busy? You'll just have to be a little patient."

"Snow White was poisoned by an apple,
Jack found a giant in his beanstalk, and look
what happened to Alice when she ate the mushroom!
And you wonder why I won't eat fruits and vegetables!?"

9
Pediatrics! You Must Be Kid-ding!

Just as our littler children (up to about three) are closer to God, sometimes the older ones seem more closely related to the other fellow! These days children have much more freedom and way less responsibility. Where better to exercise that reckless freedom than the doctor's office? So many machines that go beep, so many trolleys on wheels, so many serious grownups to annoy!

Thankfully it's a phase that passes. In the long-term we have the responsibility of making sure they grow into responsible adults. In the short-term, the least they can do in return is provide us with a few laughs!

If Only We Could Inject Manners

The pediatric nurse was giving immunization shots. Some of the little ones took them well, and others winced, but Suzy saw the needle and screamed, "No! No! No!"

"Suzy!" her embarrassed mother exclaimed. "That's not very nice."

Suzy yelled even louder, "No, thank you! No, thank you! No, thank you!"

If It Tastes So Nice—You Take It!

A mom told the family doctor, "My daughter really believes in preventative medicine."

"Does she now?" asked the doctor, remembering that he had recently written a prescription for the girl.

"Oh, yeah," Mom carried on. "Every time I try to give her any medicine she prevents it!"

Say What?

People had been telling a mom her three-year-old son was far too precocious. She didn't agree but decided to take him to the doctor anyway.

"Okay," said the doctor, "let's try some simple tests."

The boy said nothing and just sat there staring at the doctor.

"Let's assess his verbal ability," the doctor suggested. He turned to the little boy. "Can you say something? Anything. Just whatever comes into your head."

The three-year-old turned to his mom.

"Mother," he said, "do you suppose the medical practitioner would prefer logically constructed sentences or a selection of random, unconnected utterances?"

And Where Is Waldo?

A five-year-old was at the pediatrician for a checkup. As the doctor looked into her ears, he asked, "Do you think I'll find Big Bird in here?" The little girl stayed silent.

Next, the doctor took a tongue depressor and looked down her throat. He asked, "Do you think I'll find the Cookie Monster down there?" Again, the little girl was silent.

Then the doctor put a stethoscope to her

chest. As he listened to her heartbeat, he asked, "Do you think I'll hear Barney in there?"

"Oh no!" the little girl replied. "Jesus is in my heart. Barney's on my lunch box."

Me Too, Ben!

Six-year-old Ben visited the pediatrician one day. The doctor was great and addressed all of his comments and questions to young Ben.

Ben's mom smiled proudly as her son whispered all his responses into the doctor's ear. When he asked if there was anything Ben was allergic to the doctor listened to the quiet response and smiled.

It wasn't until mom visited the pharmacist to get her son's medication that she looked at the prescription and saw the doctor had written, "Not to be taken with broccoli."

Ask the Expert

An educational psychologist was reading over his notes on the plane. He was traveling to a seminar where he would address an audience of thousands on his specialty, child care.

The lady sitting next to him asked about his trip and he explained. She was very interested. Then she told him she was a grandmother with eight children, twenty grandchildren, and six great-grandchildren.

The educational psychologist sighed inwardly. This woman was bound to spend the rest of the trip trying to get free professional advice from him.

Instead, she patted his hand and nodded at his notes.

"If you get stuck with any of the hard stuff . . .just ask!"

All for Nothing

Two little boys were sitting in the doctor's waiting room. A little bored, one decided to show off.

"The pediatrician's my father," he said. "That means I get to be sick for nothing!"

The other boy wasn't impressed.

"Huh! The preacher's my father," he replied. "That means I get to be good for nothing."

Wheely?

A woman brought her elderly husband to the doctor's office in a wheelchair. As she talked to the receptionist and filled out the relevant forms, the old fellow just sat there not talking or even looking at anything much.

Then a little boy put down his building bricks and walked over to him. He put a hand on the old fellow's arm and whispered, "I know how you feel. My mom makes me go everywhere in the stroller, too."

Childproof

If you're under stress, can't stand the noise, and get a lot of headaches, do what it says on the aspirin bottle. Take two and keep away from children!

Read My Lips: "Get Out of Here!"

A woman asked the pharmacist for some vitamins for her little boy.

"Certainly," said the pharmacist. "A, B, or C?"

"I don't think it matters much," the woman replied. "He's too young to read."

The Little Darlings Grow up So Quickly

Five-year-old Carly answered the door when the census taker came by. She told him that her daddy was a doctor and he wasn't home because he had been called out to an emergency appendectomy.

"My," said the census taker, "that sure is a big word for such a little girl. Do you know what it means?"

"Sure do!" Cary said. "Four thousand bucks! And that doesn't even include the anesthesiologist!"

When You Care Enough to Send the Best

A woman was at work when the school phoned to say her daughter was sick. She went straight to the pharmacy to pick up some medicine for her daughter.

Leaving the pharmacy she realized she had locked the keys in the car. Frantic with worry she looked around and found an old rusty coat hanger that had been thrown down on the ground. She had heard of people unlocking cars with coat hangers but she had no idea how to do it. So she bowed her head and asked God to send her some help.

Within five minutes an old rusty car pulled up with a dirty, greasy, bearded man inside. The woman thought, "This is what You sent to help me?"

With no other option she explained about her daughter being sick and how she had to get the medicine to her. The man looked at her and then looked at the coat hanger. He laughed and walked over to the car. A minute later the car was opened.

She hugged him, and through her tears she said, "Thank you so much! You are a very nice man."

The man replied, "Lady, I am not a nice man. I just got out of prison today. I was in prison for car theft and have only been out for about an hour."

The woman hugged the man again and with sobbing tears cried out loud, "Oh. Thank you God! You even sent me a professional."

They *Do* Make a Tasty Snack

Five-year-old Suzie's family was getting ready for their tropical holiday. While giving them their shots the doctor told Suzie they had to be careful of diseases caused by biting insects.

"Oh, that's okay," said Suzie. "I stopped biting insects years ago."

Can You Hear the Sea?

After a day at the beach a little boy was taken to the clinic to have all the little pebbles he'd pushed into his ears removed.

When enough had been taken out for the boy to hear, the doctor asked, "Why did you stick all these pebbles in your ears?"

"Well," said the boy, "'cos they kept falling out of my nose."

I Prescribe Detention

The school nurse asked Billy what the problem was.

"It happened last night," he said. "I fell and I didn't wake up for over eight hours."

"My goodness, Billy," the nurse exclaimed. "That sounds serious. Tell me how it happened."

"I fell asleep." Billy grinned.

Bad Bee-havior

A boy went to the doctor after being stung by a bee.

"I'll put some cream on it," the doctor said.

"You'll never catch it," the boy said. "It must be miles away."

"Not the bee," the doctor said, "the place you were stung."

"Ohh," said the boy, "I was sitting under the tree by the stream."

"No, silly," the doctor said, getting exasperated. "I mean where on your body you were stung!"

By now the boy was in a lot of pain.

"It stung me on the finger!"

"Which one?"

"How should I know!" he squealed. "Bees all look the same!"

When the Eagle Screams

A frantic mom grabbed a passing nurse and demanded to know what was happening with her son.

"What's he in for?" the nurse asked.

"He swallowed a hundred dollar bill," the mom said.

"Oh yeah." The nurse remembered him. "Sorry, no change yet."

"If your life was a reality TV show, would you watch it?"

10
All in the Mind—
or Out of It!

You know the old joke, "You don't have to be mad to work here—but it helps"? Well, in an increasingly materialistic world people are often made to feel their beliefs are crazy. But look at the complexity of, say, a flower, and then wrap your head around that happening by accident! You wouldn't have to be mad to believe that—but it sure would help!

Amidst all the uncertainty two things are true. God loves us—and if we don't laugh this world might just drive us nuts! So let's be loved—and laugh. (Unless you'd rather be nuts!)

Quick Question
Q. How do psychiatrists greet each other when they haven't met for a while?

A. "You're fine. How am I?"

Detained Indefinitely
How do you tell the difference between the psychiatrists and the residents of the psychiatric hospital?

The patients are the ones who eventually get better and go home!

Mental Arithmetic
It was time for the regular capability tests. The doctor called three of his psychiatric patients into his office. After a little chitchat, he asked the first patient, "So tell me, what's three times three?"

"274," the first patient replied.

The doctor sighed and then asked the second patient the same question. "What's three times three?"

"Tuesday," the second patient replied.

"Oh dear," the doctor thought. "Looks like no one's getting out of here today."

He turned to the third patient. "What's three times three?"

The third patient tutted and said, "Obviously it's nine!"

The doctor was elated! A success!

"Just explain to the other two how you figured that out."

The third patient turned to the first patient and the second patient. "Easy," he said. "You just subtract Tuesday from 274!"

Straighten Up, and (Get Your) Fly Right

Joe was a real hypochondriac who was always convinced there was something wrong with him. He lived in fear of the serious illness he was convinced was sure to come.

One morning he staggered out of the bedroom, shouting to his wife.

"Mary! It's finally happened! I was just getting dressed, and I found I couldn't stand up straight!"

Mary rushed Joe to the doctor and waited outside while Joe was being treated. Seconds later Joe strode out the office walking as straight as ever.

"Oh, sweetheart!" Mary squealed. "The

doctor is a genius! What did he do?"

Joe blushed. "He loosened my middle shirt button from my pants buttonhole."

Quick Question

Q. Where do the wardens take their criminally insane charges for a walk?

A. Along the psycho-path.

Come and See! Oops. . .You Can't!

A man walks past the big wooden fence around the psychiatric facility. From the inside he can hear the residents chanting, "Thirteen, thirteen, thirteen!"

Curious as to what's going on he bends down and peers through a knothole.

A finger jabs him in the eye, and he staggers away shouting, "What the. . . ?"

And from the other side of the fence he hears, "Fourteen, fourteen, fourteen!"

Quick Question

Q. How many psychiatrists does it take to change a lightbulb.

A. Only one. But the light has to want to change!

True—in Your World!

The aspiring student psychiatrists from various colleges were attending their first class on emotional extremes. "First we must establish some parameters," the professor said. He turned to the student from the University of Houston. "What is the opposite of joy?"

"Sadness," replied the student.

"And the opposite of depression?" the professor asked of the student from Rice.

"Elation."

"And you," he pointed to the young man from Texas A&M. "How about the opposite of woe?"

The Aggie replied, "Sir, I believe that would be giddyap."

An "Otherwise Normal" Inspector

The county inspector was visiting the local psychiatric facility. He asked a psychiatrist, "How would you detect a mental deficiency in someone who seemed otherwise normal?"

The psychiatrist thought about it. "Well," he said, "we might try surprising them with a little lateral thinking, like. . .'Captain Cook made three voyages around the world. Which one did he die on?'"

"With all due respect," the inspector said,

"that's a dumb question. What do you do if they don't know much about history?"

You'd Be Crazy to Call

If ever you find yourself calling the psychiatric hotline you might find their answering machine responds something like this:

- "If you are obsessive-compulsive, press 1 repeatedly."
- "If you are codependent, please ask someone to press 2 for you."
- "If you have multiple personalities, press 3, 4, 5, and 6."
- "If you are paranoid, we know who you are and what you want. Stay on the line so we can trace your call."
- "If you are delusional, press 7 and your call will be transferred to the mother ship."
- "If you are schizophrenic, listen carefully and a small voice will tell you which number to press."
- "If you are manic depressive, it doesn't matter which number you press, no one will answer."
- "If you have a nervous disorder, please fidget with the hash key until someone comes on the line."

- "If you have amnesia, press 8 and state your name, address, phone number, date of birth, social security number, and your mother's maiden name."
- "If you have bipolar disorder, please leave a message after the beep, or before the beep, or after the beep."
- "If you have short-term memory loss, press 9. If you have short-term memory loss, press 9. If you have short-term memory loss, press 9. If you have short-term memory loss, press 9."
- "If you have low self-esteem, please hang up. All our operators are too busy to talk to you."

If You Have Ears to See

Two long-term patients of a psychiatric facility were called to the office to see if they were ready to rejoin society.

Harry went in first. The head psychologist asked him, "Harry, what would happen if I poked you in the eye?"

"Well, I'd be half blind," Harry responded.

"And if I poked you in the other eye?"

"I'd be completely blind."

Impressed by Harry's reasoning the psychologist congratulated him and asked him to send Mikey in.

In the waiting room Harry quickly tells Mikey the answers to the questions he'd been asked. But the psychologist changed the questions just a little.

"What would happen if I cut one of your ears off, Mikey?"

"I'd be half blind," Mikey responded with absolute certainty.

"And if I cut your other ear off?" the confused psychologist asked.

"Well, I'd be completely blind," said Mikey.

"How do you figure that, Mikey?" the psychiatrist asked.

Mike shook his head, surprised at how dumb some educated men could be. "Because my hat would fall down over my eyes, of course!"

Do the Math

What's the difference between a neurotic and a psychotic?

A psychotic thinks two plus two is five. A neurotic *knows* that two plus two is four. . .but it worries him!

You *Did* Ask

While the new patient got settled on the couch, the psychiatrist tried to get a little information.

"I'm not really aware of your situation," he said. "So perhaps you could tell me about it. Start at the very beginning."

"Of course," replied the patient. "Well, in the beginning, I created the heavens and the earth. . . ."

A Little Sleight of Mind

What's the difference between a psychologist and a magician?

A psychologist pulls habits out of rats!

Sizzling Mad!

A frustrated patient flopped down on the psychiatrist's couch.

"Doc, you have to help me. My wife is convinced I am mad just because I love sausages."

The psychiatrist was a little surprised.

"That is odd," he said. "I like a nice sausage myself."

The patient jumped excitedly to his feet and grabbed the psychiatrist's hand.

"Great! Good man! Now come and see my collection. I've got thousands of them!"

Don't Make Me Send the Sheriff Around

They do say that neurotics are people who build castles in the air and psychotics are people who live in them.

Does that mean psychiatrists are the ones who collect the rent?

Sleep Tight, Earl

Earl hadn't been sleeping well for a long time. So he finally gave in and went to see a psychiatrist.

"I just can't help it, Doc," he said. "I keep thinking there are monsters under my bed!"

"Hmm," said the psychiatrist. "A complicated problem, but I think I can cure you. It will probably mean you coming to see me every week for a year, though."

Earl wasn't too educated—but he wasn't dumb either.

"How much do you charge, Doc?"

The psychiatrist told him how much his rates were. Earl said he'd sleep on it.

Six months later the psychiatrist met Earl on the street and asked him how he was sleeping these days.

"Great, Doc!" he said. "My bartender cured me! And I took the money you would've charged me and bought a new truck!"

The psychiatrist was amazed.

"How did he do that?"

"He told me to cut the legs off my bed," Earl said. "Ain't no monsters under there now!"

You Don't *Have* to Be Mad to Work Here, But. . .

If you're tired of your job and fancy getting a psychiatric discharge, try these:

- Go to the parking lot on your lunch break and point your hairdryer at all the cars coming in and out. Watch how many slow down!
- When you get cash from the ATM jump up and down screaming, "I won! I won!"
- Page yourself over the intercom. Get increasingly annoyed when you don't answer.
- Get a CD of tropical noises. Play it from the drawer of your desk—which you will have covered with mosquito netting.
- Write in the stubs of all your checks, "For smuggling diamonds."
- When you talk to your boss end every sentence with, ". . . in accordance with the prophecy."
- When you go to lunch in the cafeteria

ask for diet water with your meal.

- Tell your boss that due to the downturn in the economy you're going to have to let him go.
- Sit a wastepaper basket on your desk. Label it, "In."
- Every time anyone asks you to do anything, say, "Would you like fries with that?"

Fantasy Uncles Can Be So Annoying!

Two psychiatrists were having a drink together, and the talk turned to their most difficult cases.

"I had a patient who lived in a pure fantasy world," said one psychiatrist. "He believed that an uncle in South America was going to die and leave him a fortune. All day long he waited for a letter to arrive from an attorney. He never went out; he never did anything. He just sat around and waited for this fantasy letter from this fantasy uncle. I worked with this man eight years."

"What was the result?" the second psychiatrist asked.

"It was an eight-year struggle. Every day for eight years, but I finally cured him."

"Well, you don't look too happy about it," the second psychiatrist commented.

"No," the first psychiatrist said. "That darned letter arrived the very next week!"

He's a Cool Guy

A woman went to her psychiatrist. "Oh, Doctor, what am I going to do? My husband thinks he's a refrigerator."

"Why exactly does that bother you?" the perplexed doctor asked.

"Oh, it doesn't usually," she said. "But when he sleeps with his mouth open at night, the light keeps me awake!"

"Every day I walk for 30 minutes, I drink 8 glasses
of water, and I eat 5 fruits and vegetables...
BUT I'M STILL GETTING OLDER!"

11
You Don't Live This Long without Learning. . . uh. . . Something. . .

Life is a test you have to fail before you can pass!
That's why some young folk are so recklessly
dumb. They're asking questions they haven't
earned the answers to yet. At the other end of
life we tend to be wiser and less reckless—even
if we secretly yearn for a little less of the former
and a little more of the latter!

Life is a test! Eventually we will be asked

what we learned. If you say it was about God and love you'll get a passing grade. I'm guessing an "A."

But here are a few less serious answers. . . .

Two Out of Three Ain't Bad

Frank had been quite the ladies' man and player all his life, but now that he was getting up there in age, his doctor was getting concerned about him.

"Frank," the doctor said, "I can add fifteen more years to your life if you will just give up the wine, women, and song."

Frank thought for a few minutes, then said, "Tell you what doc, I'll settle for five more years and just give up singing."

For Gifts That Matter

A couple who had been courting for many decades finally decided to get married. Their first stop was the local pharmacy. They asked the pharmacist if he stocked heart medication. "Of course," he replied.

"How about pills for circulation?" they asked.

"Yup," the pharmacist said.

"How about medication for rheumatism?"

"Of course!"

"Pills for the memory?"

"Uh-huh," the slightly confused pharmacist replied.

"Vitamins?"

"Sure do."

"Viagra?" the old man whispered.

"Even that," the pharmacist reassured him.

"Excellent," the old lady said. "In that case we would like to register here for our wedding gifts!"

Doctor's Orders

Pete and Mike were playing checkers in the park. Pete asked Mike how his last doctor's appointment had gone.

"Oh, just fine," said Mike. "He told me that at my age any additional stress could kill me."

"How's that fine?" Pete wanted to know.

"Well," said Mike, "when his bill arrived I had the perfect excuse for shredding it."

Have You Heard about Fred?

Fred's hearing had been deteriorating for many years. One day his doctor told him about a new, miniature, flesh-colored aid that would give him perfect hearing. Fred could try it out if he liked.

A month later Fred returned and he was delighted with the improvement!

"I'm so pleased," the doctor said. "And your family, they must be delighted, too."

"Hmm," said Fred, "I haven't mentioned it to them yet. I've just been catching up on the stuff I missed all these years. I've changed my will five times in the last four weeks!"

What Memory Clinic?

Two elderly couples were sitting on a park bench, feeding the ducks.

"Hey, Jack," one guy said to the other. "How was the memory clinic you went to last month?"

"Outstanding," Jack replied. "They taught me all the latest psychological techniques: visualization, association, etcetera. It was great."

"Fantastic!" the other guy said. "And what was the name of the clinic?"

Jack went blank. He thought and thought, but couldn't remember. So he tried some of the techniques he had been taught. A smile spread across his face, and he asked his friend, "What do you call that flower with the long stem and thorns?"

"You mean a rose?"

"Yes, that's it!" He turned to his wife. "Rose, what was the name of that memory clinic?"

Stick with That Treatment

A woman shuffles into a doctor's office. She's bent over and leaning on a walking stick.

Ten minutes later she comes out again looking half her age and walking upright. A man in the waiting room who had seen her go in said, "Wow! What did the doctor do for you?"

The woman said, "Nothing much. He just gave me a longer walking stick."

Twist and Creak

The doctor had recommended a gentle course of exercise to an elderly woman. After the first class she came back to the doctor's office.

"How did it go?" he asked.

"Well," she said, "I bent, I straightened, I hopped, I twisted, I spun. . .but by the time I'd gotten my leotard on the class was finished!"

Things Are Much Heavier These Days

An older couple walked into the doctor's office. She was still quite sprightly. He was doubled over and walked with a lot of pain.

"Oh," the new doctor said, sizing him up at once. "Arthritis? With complications?"

"No," the wife replied. "Building a garage. With concrete blocks."

And Again Afterward

The doctor asked Sam what the problem was.

"It's my memory, Doc," Sam said. "I park the car to go shopping—I can't remember where I left it. I go upstairs—and can't remember what I'm up there for. I go to a nearby town—and can't remember my way back. Is there anything I can do?"

"Sure is," said the doctor. "You can pay me in advance!"

Ahhh, I See!

Due to be discharged from the hospital, the elderly woman wasn't going to go quietly.

"Someone stole my wig while I was under the anesthetic," she shouted.

The doctor tried to calm her.

"Madam, I can assure you none of my staff would have done such a thing."

"I can assure you someone must have," she insisted. "When I came to I found a cheap and nasty wig on my bedside table instead of the lovely one I came in with."

"Might I suggest, madam," the doctor said calmly, "that your cataract operation was more successful than you expected?"

Not the Brightest Light

Grandma Jackson was just plain cantankerous. She'd never been sick in eighty years and really resented having to go to the hospital. She complained to her family on the way, she complained to the receptionist, she complained to the nurse and the doctor, she even complained to the orderly who wheeled her to her room.

Ignoring her moans with almost saintly patience, the orderly got her tucked up in bed. He explained where all her stuff was, showed her how to work the TV remote, and told her he would pop by later just to see how she was.

As he was about to leave, Grandma Jackson asked him what the cable with a button on the end looped over the head of her bed was.

"Oh," said the orderly. "That's in case you need anything in the night."

"Does it ring a bell?" she asked.

"No," the orderly replied. "It turns on a light in the hall for the nurse on duty."

"Huh!" said Grandma Jackson indignantly. "If I'm so sick, the night nurse can darn well turn on her own light to get here!"

You Walked How Far?

A seventy-eight-year-old man went in for a physical. The doctor examined him and said,

"You have the body of a fifty-year-old. How do you do it?"

"Well, Doc," he said. "The wife and I married near on sixty years ago. We decided that whenever we had an argument she would cool off in the kitchen and I would take a walk."

"Uh-huh?" said the doctor, still not getting it.

"I guess," said the man, "you can put my good health down to my spending a lot of time outdoors!"

You're Only as Young as Your Joints Feel

Fred shuffled into the doctor's office.

"Doc, you need to do something," he said. "My knee hurts!"

"Fred," the doctor sighed, "you're 105 you have to expect your knee to hurt at that age!"

"And you are a hopeless doctor," Fred retorted. "That's a ridiculous diagnosis!"

"How do you mean?" the surprised doctor asked.

"Well, my other knee's exactly the same age—and it doesn't hurt!"

Mind Me Now, Walter!

"It's bad news, I'm afraid," the doctor told old Walt. "There's nothing I can do for your wife.

Her mind is completely gone."

"I'm not really surprised, Doc," said Walt. "She's been giving me a piece of it every day for the last sixty years. I'm just amazed it lasted this long!"

Spider Granny

A ninety-year-old lady went to the doctor after she twisted her knee. The doctor bandaged it and told her she would need to be careful if her knee was to heal completely.

"No climbing up and down stairs for the next two weeks," the doctor warned.

Two weeks later she came back, and the doctor was delighted to see her knee had healed perfectly.

"Does this mean I can go upstairs now?" she asked.

"Certainly," the doctor said.

"Good," she replied. "A woman my age has her dignity to think of, and I can't tell you how foolish I've felt climbing up and down the drainpipe."

An Added Incentive

An old man was about to undergo surgery. But he wasn't worried. He knew he was in good hands because the surgeon was his son. But still, he wasn't taking any chances.

As the anesthetist was about to put him out he waved his son over.

"What is it, dad?" the surgeon asked.

"I just wanted you to know," the old man said, "that if anything goes wrong. . ."

"Oh, dad," the surgeon said. "Nothing will go wrong."

"It better not for your sake, son," the old man said. "Because if I die your mother is coming to live with you and your wife!"

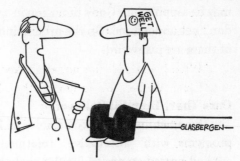

"That's all the alternative medicine your HMO will pay for."

12
Alternative Therapies, You're Wonderful!

Most of the medicines we take today originally came from nature. Sadly, we're getting rid of nature before fully exploring it. It's just possible the cure for everything is out there, either growing in the ground or wafting through the air. . .or some would say in our auras!

God made us to live in this world. By the time we arrived the world had already been prepared for us, most likely with all we would ever need. Some of the more unusual "complimentary" or "alternative" therapies may be tapping into God's provision in a way we don't yet understand. On the other hand, some of them are just weird!

Cure That, Then I'll Believe!

The therapist insisted he could solve *all* Frank's problems with "alternative" treatments. He applied heated stones to Frank's chakras, gave him a seaweed wrap, acupuncture to the soles of his feet, hypnotherapy, and burned scented herbal candles in his ears.

It was no use.

When Frank went outside his car still wouldn't start!

Spinally!

Bill had suffered from back problems for years. He'd tried all kinds of treatments to no avail. Reaching the point where he could hardly walk straight, he finally consulted a chiropractor. Right from the outset he told the chiropractor he thought he was a quack and that this treatment, like all the others, was bound to fail.

Amazingly though, it worked!

"How do you feel about what we do now?" the chiropractor asked.

A little shamefaced, Bill replied, "I stand corrected."

Could I Have a Repeat Prescription, Please?

An alternative therapist came up with a new substance to help men who wanted to undergo a sex change. Instead of treating them with hormones he used a mystery liquid to "feminize" his patients. It caused them to. . .

- put on weight
- talk excessively (while making no sense to their partner)
- get excessively emotional
- become hopeless drivers
- cry a lot
- love everyone
- and become annoyingly irrational

An investigation by medical authorities closed him down when they discovered the mystery liquid was beer!

Herbal Medicine

Paramedics wheeled an unconscious hippie into the hospital. The doctor on call looked at the patient. There were no obvious clues, so he asked the hippie's friends what the problem was.

"Drugs?" he asked. "LSD? Coke? Cannabis?"

"Yeah, man, yeah," a friend said. "All that stuff. But then we ran out and had to make our own."

"What do you mean, you made your own?" the astonished doctor asked.

"We. . .kinda. . .like, raided the spice rack to make a joint," the embarrassed friend told him. "There was some ginger, garlic, chilies, coriander, a little ground coconut. . . ."

"That explains it," the doctor said to the paramedics. "He's in a korma!"

Then and Now

In 2,000 BC a man had a headache. The shaman said, "Eat this root."

In AD 1,000 the priest said, "That root is heathen; recite this chant."

In AD 1800 the apothecary said, "That chant is superstition; drink this potion."

In AD 1900 the chemist said, "That potion is hokum; take this pill."

In AD 1960 the doctor said, "That pill doesn't work; take this antibiotic."

In AD 2000 the alternative practitioner

said, "That antibiotic is man-made. Here—eat this root!"

True Happiness Was There All the Time

Janie's lifestyle guru told his class that the secret of happiness was completion. Once she had completed all the things she had started in life but left unfinished, then she would find true happiness.

So, she went home from the class. She finished a bottle of Chardonnay, a bottle of Merlot, a cheesecake, a packet of Oreos, a block of chocolates, and a romance novel.

You have no idea how happy she felt!

By Any Other Name

What do you call an alternative medicine that works?

Medicine!

Enough to Give You a Real Headache!

Billy had suffered from migraine headaches on and off for most of his adult life. He had tried every kind of medication available but nothing made any difference. Eventually he tried a complimentary healer.

The healer sympathized. He, too, had suffered from migraines and knew how useless conventional medicine was for them.

"I still get them occasionally," he told Billy. "But here's how I make them go away. I go to my house. I run a hot bath with scented oils. I put on some Beethoven, and I pour myself a glass of wine. No cheap stuff. It can only be the most expensive wine available. Then I lie in the bath, breathe in the aromas, savor the wine, and let the music soothe my pains away."

Impressed, Billy promised to try it.

A month later he came back, and he couldn't thank the therapist enough. "I had a couple of migraines," he said, "but I treated them as you said, and they went away. Oh by the way, doc, you're running low on scented oils—but you sure do have a lovely house!"

The Alphabet Cure

A man went to see the doctor.

"And how can I help you?" the doctor asked. But the man didn't open his mouth. Instead he handed the doctor a note explaining that he had a psychological condition that meant he couldn't speak.

The doctor thought this would be the perfect opportunity to try some "alternative" therapy. So he leaned forward and poked the man in the eye.

"Aaaaaaaaaaaaaaaaaaaaa!" the man yelled.

"Well done," the doctor said. "Come back tomorrow, and we'll try B."

Remember This?

A new healer arrived in town. He brought with him an incredible reputation for healing people with his homemade remedies. Zeke wasn't convinced. So he visited the healer's tent and said, "Cure me, Doc. I've lost my sense of taste."

The healer muttered to himself, dug into some boxes, consulted some scrolls, and brought out a jar marked 87. He poured out a spoonful of liquid and told Zeke to take it.

Zeke swallowed it down—then spit it out. He ran out of the tent and washed his mouth out in a horse trough. "That's disgusting!" he shouted.

The healer shouted after him, "Congratulations on getting your sense of taste back, sir!"

Zeke was determined not to be beaten. He'd heard about the problems modern medical science was having with memory loss, so he went back to the healer and said, "Doc, I've lost my memory."

"I have the very remedy," the healer said, and brought out a jar marked 87.

Zeke left the tent flaps flying in the wind!

"You remembered!" the healer shouted after him.

Well, Medicine Bottles Are Expensive

A backwoods doc was visited by a big-city physician. The city guy couldn't get over the lovely house and up-to-date surgery the country guy had. Over a few drinks the country guy revealed his secret.

"My wife and I have a vegetable garden out back. We grow all kinds of things there, juice them, and bottle them."

"Are they medicinal?" the city guy asked.

"Not at all," the country guy confided. "But what we do is wait until folks round here go on vacation. When they come back I tell them they don't look so great. They usually say their vacation really took it out of them. So I sell them a bottle of my tonic, and a few weeks after that, I tell them how much better they're looking.

"A month or so after that I tell them they are looking terrible. When they come to buy more tonic I ask them to bring a urine sample. That way I even get my bottles back!"

Aww, Nuts!

A practitioner of alternative medicine put great faith in the healing powers of berries and nuts. So much so that each evening after he got home he would visit his local bar for a hazelnut daiquiri to help him wind down.

After a while the bartender got used to the doctor's routine, and he would have the drink waiting on the bar for him when he arrived.

But then came the day when the bartender ran out of hazelnut extract, so he whipped up a quick concoction using hickory nuts instead.

The doctor came in and found the drink waiting for him. He took a sip and spluttered all over the bar.

"This isn't a hazelnut daiquiri," he exclaimed.

"You're right," the shamefaced bartender admitted. "It's not hazelnut. It's a hickory daiquiri, Doc."

A Different Kind of Complimentary

A pretty young woman rushed to the doctor's office in some distress. After a quick examination the doctor said. "You have acute appendicitis."

"That's sweet of you, Doc," the woman replied. "But I can get compliments anywhere. I came here looking for medical help!"

Final, Final, Final Demand

A medical doctor and a natural healer were arguing over a new herbal remedy.

"So what does it cure?" the doctor asked.

The healer reeled off a list of illnesses this new remedy cured, but the doctor said there were already existing medicines for all of them.

"I still don't understand why you like this stuff so much," the doctor said.

"Well the best bit," the healer said, grinning, "is in the side effects."

"Yeah, like what?"

"It causes short-term memory loss."

"How can that be a good thing?" the doctor yelled.

"It is *so* good," the healer insisted. "Seven of my patients have paid me at least three times this month!"

Dumb Advice Indeed

"I've been seeing a faith healer for this problem," the man confessed to the doctor, "but he couldn't do anything for me."

"A faith healer!" the doctor said scornfully. "How stupid can some people be? And what ridiculous, dumb advice did this uneducated charlatan give you?"

"We–ell, doc." The man hesitated. "He told me to come and see you."

Naturally

A young woman set up in business as an herbal healer. All of her medicines were made from the stems and tubers of plants growing naturally in the area.

All her family and friends were rooting for her!

Line Up to Be Punctured

Ahhh, acupuncture! That's a jab well done!

How Would You Bill a Cranberry?

Patient: "Do you think cranberries are healthy?

Doctor: "Well, I've never had one come to me with a problem, so. . . ."

Now This *Will* Hurt

Q: Why did the guru refuse novocaine when he went to his dentist?

A: He wanted to transcend dental medication.

"I already diagnosed myself on the Internet. I either have three left kidneys, recurring puberty, or Dutch Elm disease."

13
Room for Emergencies!

"If you have a problem, if no one else can help, and if you can find them. . ." That was the introduction to the cult eighties TV program *The A-Team*. But the guys who are really going to save your life in dramatic circumstances are the emergency room team! Often they are the stop of last resort for problems no one else wants to deal with.

But if you have a problem even they can't deal with, go to the God team. If His people can't deal with it, He will personally. And He loves it when a plan comes together!

Virtually a Hunk

A man and an older woman walk into the emergency room after a minor accident. When the nurse asks his details he informs her that he is six feet tall and 185 pounds.

The confused receptionist looks over the desk and sees a man both shorter and heavier than that description.

Just then his mom leans over and whispers to him, "Sweetheart, this is the ER, not the Internet."

It's an Emergency—I've Lost a Number!

Shortly after the 911 emergency number was introduced an elderly lady appeared in a hospital emergency room. She was really ill, but she had driven herself to the hospital, narrowly avoiding several accidents, and had barely managed to stagger in from the parking lot.

The horrified nurse said, "Why didn't you call the 911 number and get an ambulance to pick you up?

"Well, I would have," she said. "But the numbers on my phone don't go up to eleven!"

What Do We Want? Uhh. . .I Dunno

The ER department of a major hospital went on strike. Aware of how bad it would look in the press, the hospital administrators were anxious to sort it out. But still the ambulances were backed up along the road!

A reporter grabbed an administrator and asked him why he wasn't giving the ER staff what they wanted.

"We want to!" the administrator shouted. "But we can't find a pharmacist to read their posters for us!"

You Might Be an ER Doc If. . .

- your favorite hallucinogen is exhaustion.
- discussing dismemberment over a gourmet meal seems perfectly normal to you.
- you think that caffeine should be available in IV form.
- you get an almost irresistible urge to stand and wolf down your food even in the nicest restaurants.
- you say to yourself "great veins" when looking at complete strangers.
- you believe that unspeakable evils will befall you if anyone says, "Boy, it is quiet around here."

- you have ever referred to someone's death as a transfer to the "Eternal Care Unit."
- your most common assessment question is "What changed tonight to make it an emergency after six (hours, days, weeks, months, years)?"

I Remember When

An elderly lady was brought into a New York hospital's emergency room. After assessing her, the doctor decided that surgery would be necessary. Trying to reassure her he asked if she had ever had surgery before.

"Ohh. . .yes," she said. "But it was a long, long time ago. I can't really remember what it was for."

The sharp-eyed doc had spotted an old scar on her abdomen.

"Is this where you had the surgery?" he asked.

"No," she said. "It was in San Francisco. "See, I'm not completely forgetful!"

Chainsaw Surgery

Bubba and Duke were out cutting wood when Bubba slipped. His chainsaw sliced his arm off.

Duke, who watched a lot of medical dramas on TV, knew just what to do. He wrapped Bubba's arm in a plastic bag, bundled the arm and Bubba into his truck, and took them both to the nearest emergency room.

The ER doctor praised Duke's quick thinking. "Reattaching arms is difficult," he said, "but you've given your friend the best possible chance. I'll see what I can do now."

The doctor did amazing work, and a few months later Bubba was as good as new and out cutting wood again. Then an unexpected twitch in his arm swung the chainsaw, and it sliced Bubba's leg off.

Duke did his thing again. He wrapped the leg in a plastic bag and helped Bubba hop to the truck.

The doctor told Duke he did the right thing. He went to work, and Bubba got almost complete use of his leg back.

Back out in the woods months later, hobbling on his reattached leg and the chainsaw swinging from his reattached arm, Bubba accidentally cut his own head off.

Duke just took it in his stride. With Bubba's torso in the passenger seat and his head in the plastic bag Duke drove the well-worn trail to the hospital.

He reckoned heads would be the hardest

thing to reattach, but even so, he was stunned when the doctor told him Bubba didn't make it. He was even more amazed when the surgeon told him it was his fault Bubba died.

"But you always told me I did the right thing!" Duke said. "And I thought you could reattach anything."

"Well, maybe I could have," the doctor replied. "But you didn't put any air holes in that plastic bag—and poor Bubba suffocated!"

Forget about the Cast, Buy Me Lunch Instead

A man hobbled into the ER complaining about his leg. The doctor laid him on a gurney and examined the leg. Not finding anything obvious he put his stethoscope to the man's thigh. A little voice said, "Hey, Doc, can you spare ten bucks?"

Startled, he put the stethoscope to the man's shin. "Buddy, can you spare the price of a cup of coffee?" another little voice said.

The doctor staggered back in shock. But then realization dawned.

"Oh, it's not so bad after all," he told the man. "It's just. . .your leg's broke in two places."

Not Exactly Helping

Two hunters were out in the woods when one of them collapsed. The other guy took out his cell phone and called 911. "My friend is dead!" he said. "What can I do?"

"Keep calm," the operator said. "I can help you. Now, first let's make sure he's dead."

There was a silence and then a shot. Back on the phone, the guy said: "Okay, now what?"

I'll Never Eat in the ER Again!

A snooty waitress from an upscale restaurant collapsed and had to be rushed to the ER. Being a Saturday evening the ER was packed full. The waitress was lifted onto a gurney and left alone.

An hour later she saw a doctor walking along the corridor. She recognized him from the restaurant—and he recognized her.

"Doctor," she gasped, "I've been waiting an hour. . . ."

"Sorry, ma'am," the doctor replied. "That's not my table."

Bug Out

The ER nurse examined their latest casualty. He looked as if he had been beaten up.

"Who did this to you?" she asked.

"You are never going to believe this," the man said. "I was sitting at home, minding my own business, when the doorbell rang. I opened the door, and a six-foot cockroach punched me in the face. I fell over, and it started kicking me!"

"I do believe it," the nurse said. "You're the third guy we've had in tonight with the same story!"

"Yeah," said a doctor, walking by. "There's quite a nasty bug going around."

How to Stew a Doctor

The ER doc was dealing with a woman who had just been brought in. Working frantically to make sure she was okay, he tried to make conversation with her, both to keep her calm and to reassure himself she was still okay.

"Don't I recognize you?" he asked at one point.

The woman didn't think so, but she said she worked at Mercy Hospital on the other side of the city.

"Ahh, that's it! I was at Mercy for six months

three or four years ago. Tell me," he said, trying to lighten the mood, "is the food still as truly awful there as it was back then?"

Just then the woman's heart gave out and she died.

A moment later another doctor walked past and saw her lying there.

"Oh hey," he said. "I recognize her. Wasn't she was the head cook over at Mercy?"

Time for a Career Change

Paramedics wheeled a man into the ER on a gurney. He had broken legs, broken arms, broken ribs, and skull fracture. Trying to get his details while the doctors were doing their bit, the receptionist asked him his name.

"Dave," he said.

"And your occupation, Dave?"

"Well," he thought for a moment, "I used to be a window cleaner."

Thinking the cracked skull had confused him a little the receptionist played along.

"Oh, and when did you give that up?"

"About halfway down," said Dave.

Car Sharing

A father brought his nine-year-old son into the ER.

"He has a toy car stuck up his nose," the father said. "Can you imagine anything so dumb?"

The ER doc refrained from comment, and after applying lubricant, forceps, and some gentle wiggling, the toy car was removed from the embarrassed boy's nostril. The boy reached for his toy, but his father snatched it first.

"Oh no, you don't!" he said. "You can't be trusted not to do something stupid with it. I'll keep it safe."

Two hours later the dad came back to the ER by himself.

"Did you forget something?" the doctor asked.

"No," said the father, blushing. "Do you remember my boy had a toy car up his nose? Well, I just couldn't see how he managed to get it up there. And now. . .well. . .do you have any more of that lubricant?"

If Only Her Husband Hadn't Had Fleas

A woman ran into the emergency room shouting for help.

"I'll help," said a doctor. "What's the problem?"

"Doctor," she gasped. "It's my husband. He thinks he's a dog!"

The doctor backed off and raised his hands.

"Ma'am," he said, "I am an emergency-room trauma surgeon. I think your husband would be better off with a psychiatrist."

"You don't understand," she insisted. "You are just the man he needs! You see, he was scratching his fleas on the driveway when I reversed the SUV over him!"

Toe the Line, Chuck

Chuck limped into the ER with a broken toe. The ER was really busy. A nurse took him by the elbow and led him into an examination bay.

"Strip off," she said, "and I'll be back when I get a chance."

"Strip off?" Chuck yelled. "Why do I need to strip off to have my toe examined?"

"Hospital policy," the nurse said as she pulled the curtain closed and disappeared.

"That's a ridiculous policy!" Chuck said.

"Hey man," came a voice from the next bay. "If I have to do it you have to do it. I only came in to check the telephones!"

**"I can't help you unless you're more specific.
Now are you feeling 'yucky' or are you feeling 'icky'?"**

14
Deciphering Doctor-ese

These days if you live in an American city there's a good chance you know a few words in two or three different languages. But there's more to understanding each other than just speaking the same language. Take a parent talking to a teenager. Take a wife talking to her husband. Take God talking to His creation. Take our doctor speaking to "Ordinary Joe."

Talking is one thing; listening and understanding are different things again. What the doc says and what Joe hears are. . . well. . .let's just hope we understand God (or our spouses, or our children) better than Joe understands "doctor-ese!"

Doc says, "Adenoma."
Joe hears, "What you say to your mom
    when you don't know."

Doc says, "Alimentary."
Joe hears, "What Holmes said to Watson."

Doc says, "Anally."
Joe hears, "Happening once a year."

Doc says, "Antibody."
Joe hears, "Someone who is just against
    stuff."

Doc says, "Artery."
Joe hears, "The study of paintings."

Doc says, "Bacteria."
Joe hears, "The café at the back."

Doc says, "Barium."
Joe hears, "What you do when CPR doesn't
    work."

Doc says, "Benign."
Joe hears, "What you be after you be
    eight."

Doc says, "Caesarean section."
Joe hears, "A neighborhood in Rome."

Doc says, "Cardiology."
Joe hears, "An advanced study of poker
    playing."

Doc says, "Carpal."
Joe hears, "Someone you drive to work
    with."

Doc says, "Castrate."
Joe hears, "The market price for setting a
    fracture."

Doc says, "Cat scan."
Joe hears, "Searching for kitty."

Doc says, "Cauterize."
Joe hears, "Making eye contact with a girl."

Doc says, "Chiropractor."
Joe hears, "Egyptian doctor."

Doc says, "Coma."
Joe hears, "A punctuation mark."

Doc says, "Congenital."
Joe hears, "Friendly."

Doc says, "Coronary."
Joe hears, "A domesticated yellow bird."

Doc says, "Cystogram."
Joe hears, "A cable sent to your sister."

Doc says, "Dilate."
Joe hears, "Live long."

Doc says, "Dislocation."
Joe hears, "Around here."

Doc says, "Fibula."
Joe hears, "A little lie."

Doc says, "Genital."
Joe hears, "Not Jewish."

Doc says, "Hangnail."
Joe hears, "A coat hook."

Doc says, "Hernia."
Joe hears, "She's nearby."

Doc says, "Herpes."
Joe hears, "What a woman does in the ladies' room."

Doc says, "Hippocampus."
Joe hears, "A school for hippopotami."

Doc says, "ICU."
Joe hears he's lost that game of hide and seek.

Doc says, "Impotent."
Joe hears, "Well-known and influential."

Doc says, "Inpatient."
Joe hears, "Someone who is tired of waiting."

Doc says, "Intern."
Joe hears, "One after the other."

Doc says, "Intestine."
Joe hears, "Currently taking an exam."

Doc says, "Labor pains."
Joe hears, "An injury at work."

Doc says, "Lactose."
Joe hears, "Someone with no toes."

Doc says, "Lymph."
Joe hears, "Walk gingerly."

Doc says, "Medical staff."
Joe hears, "A doctor's walking stick."

Doc says, "Microbes."
Joe hears, "Small dressing gowns."

Doc says, "Minor operation."
Joe hears, "Digging coal."

Doc says, "Morbid."
Joe hears, "A higher offer."

Doc says, "Nitrates."
Joe hears, "Cheaper than day rates."

Doc says, "Node."
Joe hears, "Was aware of."

Doc says, "Obesity."
Joe hears, "A city where fat people live."

Doc says, "Outpatient."
Joe hears, "Someone under anesthetic."

Doc says, "Pacemaker."
Joe hears, "Winner of a Nobel Prize."

Doc says, "Postoperative."
Joe hears, "Mailman."

Doc says, "Proteins."
Joe hears, "People in favor of teenagers."

Doc says, "Recovery Room."
Joe hears, "A place to do upholstery."

Doc says, "Red blood count."
Joe hears, "Dracula."

Doc says, "Rheumatic."
Joe hears, "Bringing your sweetheart
    flowers."

Doc says, "Saline."
Joe hears, "What you do on a boat."

Doc says, "Scar."
Joe hears, "Something you smoke."

Doc says, "Seizure."
Joe hears, "A Roman emperor."

Doc says, "Terminal illness."
Joe hears, "Getting sick at the airport."

Doc says, "Tibia."
Joe hears, "A country in North Africa."

Doc says, "Tumor."
Joe hears, "Another two."

Doc says, "Ultrasound."
Joe hears, "A really loud noise."

Doc says, "Urine."
Joe hears, "The opposite of you're out."

Doc says, "Varicose."
Joe hears, "Nearby."

Doc says, "Vein."
Joe hears, "Conceited."

Doc says, "Weak."
Joe hears, "Seven days."

And What the Doctors Really Mean When They Say. . .

"Well, what have we here?"

(He has no idea, and he's hoping you're going to give him a clue.)

"Let's see what develops."

(If you wait long enough it might turn into something he can cure.)

"How are we today?"

(He feels fine. You look like an interesting case!)

"I'd like to prescribe a new drug."

("I'd like to write a paper on how this drug works.")

"If it doesn't clear up in a week, make another appointment."

(He has no idea what it is, and he's hoping it will go away by itself.)

"That's a nasty-looking wound!"

("Don't bleed on my carpet!")

"This may nip a little."

("Hold on tight. This is really gonna hurt!")

"Well, we're not doing so well today, are we?"
(He can't remember your name or why you're there.)

"Hmm, there's a lot of it going around."
(And as soon as you leave I'm going on the Internet to find out all about it!)

"I'd like to run some more tests."
("Maybe the lab guys can diagnose this for me.")

"Let's check your medical history."
(He wants to see if you paid your last bill.)

"Well, I have some good news and some bad news."
(The good news is he's gonna buy that new sports car. The bad news is—you're paying!)

"I'd like my associate to have a look at you."
(He's having a tough time and could do with a good laugh.)

"Everything seems to be fine."
(Drat!)

"I want you to follow a healthy lifestyle...
whatever the experts say that is this week."

15
Generally Practicing

You might think that being a specialist is much harder than being a general practitioner. Just as being a pastor or evangelical speaker *seems* more difficult than being an ordinary man or woman of faith. These specialties might require more in-depth knowledge, but the general practitioner, whether he or she be in faith or medicine, has to deal with. . .well. . .anything at any time.

Specialists are wonderful at what they do, but the general practitioner has to be on top of his game, spiritually and medically, all the time! Maybe that's why we all need so much general practice!

Honest, Honey, I Have a Severe Case of Gobbledygook

The patient was complaining that he just wasn't capable of doing all the things around the house that he used to. The doctor gave him a thorough checkup, and he prepared himself for the bad news.

"So hit me with it, Doc. In plain English, what's the problem?"

"Okay," the doctor said. "In plain English you are fine, just bone idle."

The man rocked back but made a quick recovery.

"Okay, Doc. Now give it to me in medical Latin so I can tell my wife."

Philosoph-itis

The stranger was checking into the local hotel, and the receptionist noticed he put "Dr." before his name on the register.

"If it's not too impertinent a question," she

said, "what kind of doctor are you?"

The stranger put the pen down. "Actually," he said, "I'm a doctor of philosophy."

"Wow!" said the receptionist. "I can't recall we ever had a case of that around here."

That's Old!

You know your doctor is too old when you look at the framed diploma on his wall and realize his Hippocratic Oath was signed by Hippocrates!

Key Please, Nurse

Old Doc Wilson meant well but was a little past his prime. But he still made house calls!

He was called to a home where the wife was in terrible pain. Doc Wilson shut the bedroom door while he examined her. A minute later he came out and asked her startled husband for a hammer. Nervously, the husband supplied the hammer. A minute later Doc Wilson was back out asking for a screwdriver. Almost out of his mind with worry the husband handed over a screwdriver. But when Doc Wilson came back out a minute later and asked for a hacksaw the husband cracked.

"Please, Doc, tell me what's wrong with my wife!"

"Oh," Doc Wilson looked surprised. "I don't know. I haven't been able to get my bag open yet."

A Promise Kept

Two men sat comparing operation stories. "The doctor said he would have me on my feet in two weeks," said the first guy.

"And did he?" his friend asked.

"Yup," the first guy said. "I had to sell the car to pay his bill."

A Whole-Life Treatment

Two men got talking in a coffee shop. One was new in town.

"This looks like a really healthy place," he said.

"It sure is," said the local man. "When I came here I couldn't say a word. I had hardly any hair on my head. I couldn't walk two steps, and I had to be lifted out of bed."

"Wow!" said the new guy. "How long have you been here?"

"Oh," said the local man. "I was born here."

Yeah, Why Not?

The doctor warned the wife that her husband was highly contagious. "He's best left here at home, but you will have to sterilize everything he used. Boil his cutlery, his cup, his plates. Regularly change his bed linen, and boil the sheets every time."

The woman's daughter wasn't very impressed by this advice. When the doctor left she tugged at her mom's arm and said, "Why not just boil daddy and get rid of all the germs at once?"

"Real" Headlines in Medical Journals

- New Study of Obesity Looks for Larger Test Group
- New Vaccine May Contain Rabies
- Hospitals Are Sued by Seven Foot Doctors
- Kids Make Nutritious Snacks
- Eye Drops Off Shelf
- Man Minus Ear Waives Hearing

And the Chief Doctor Was God

You know your doctor is old when he recalls his days at Mount Sinai and mentions that one of his "colleagues" was called Moses!

Not Just a Pretty Face

A man passed out on a busy sidewalk. An attractive, well-dressed young woman stopped to help him. But a jock gently moved her aside.

"I've had first-aid training, sweetheart," he said. He started doing some basic stuff like removing the man's tie, loosening his belt. All the while he was looking at the woman, flashing his grin and explaining to her what he was doing. Despite his efforts it was apparent the man wasn't getting better. In fact he was getting worse.

The jock carried on regardless, assuring her he had it all under control. But eventually his cool facade began to crumble.

"I loosened his clothing. . . . I checked his airway. . .I. . .I. . ."

"Yes," said the woman. "And now you're at the part where you call a real doctor. And look, here I am!"

Cure These!

A guy walked into a doctor's office. The receptionist asked him what he had. "Shingles," he replied

She took down his name, address, and insurance number and told him to have a seat.

A few minutes later a nurse's aid came out

and asked him what he had. "Shingles."

So she took down his height, weight, and a complete medical history and told him to wait in the examining room.

Ten minutes later a nurse came in and asked him what he had.

"Shingles," he repeated a little irately.

She gave him a blood test, a blood pressure test, and an electrocardiogram and told him to take off all his clothes and wait for the doctor.

Fifteen minutes later the doctor came in and asked him what he had.

"Shingles!" he shouted.

"Oh! Yes?" The doctor was a little taken aback.

"Yes!" the guy insisted. "They're outside in the truck. Where do you want them?"

The Mower the Merrier

A couple driving through a residential area saw a man passed out by his front door. Immediately they called the paramedics. They arrived, scooped the man up, and rushed him to the hospital.

As the man recovered consciousness in the hospital he was confronted by bewildered doctors. "To be honest," they said, "the best we can determine is that, well, you simply fainted."

"I'll say I did," the man replied. "And you would have too! My teenage son asked for the key to the garage and came out riding the lawn mower!"

A Good Excuse, Actually
Jake walked into the doctor's office.

"Ah, Jake," the doctor said, "I haven't seen you for quite a while."

"Sorry about that, Doc," Jake said. "I've been ill."

A Team-Building Illness
The patient told the doctor he had a sore throat and a temperature. "But the funny thing is," he croaked, "everybody at work seems to have exactly the same thing!"

"Ahh!" said the doctor, nodding wisely. "Sounds like a staff infection to me!"

Ring, Ring, Is Anyone There?
A young doctor had just opened his office and was really full of his own importance. His secretary told him a man was there to see him. He told her to send him in.

Trying to impress his first patient by how

busy and important he was, he picked up the phone. "Yes, that's right," he said. "What's that, senator? Yes, I can cure that. No, you have to come to me. I'll expect you ten past two. Alright. No later mind. I'm a very busy man."

He hung up and turned to the man waiting. "What can I do for you?"

"It's what I can do for you," the man said. "I just came in to connect the phone."

A Country Gentleman

The receptionist examined the patient information that had just been handed to her. Zeb had filled in all his personal details, but the section marked "Complaint" had been left empty.

When she asked him why he hadn't filled it in Zeb gave the receptionist his most charming grin.

"Shucks, ma'am. I've only been here but ten minutes, and you've been real nice! I ain't got no complaints at all."

An Aurrible Joke

The doctor was carrying out a thorough examination. He wanted the instrument that helped him look in the patient's ears, but the new nurse had arranged his instruments tray differently.

"For goodness' sake, nurse," he snapped. "Give me my auroscope!"

"But doctor," the surprised nurse replied, "I don't even know your star sign!"

Doctor on Call?

A young man was running up and down the main street shouting, "Call me a doctor! Somebody call me a doctor!"

A woman ran over to him.

"Are you ill? Are you hurt? What's the matter with you?" she asked.

"Nothing's the matter," the young man reassured her.

"Then why do you want me to call you a doctor?" she asked.

"Because I just passed all my medical exams!"

*+~["^:<#>

A man went to his doctor for a checkup. The doctor completed his examination and wrote out a prescription for him, in his usual illegible writing.

The patient put it in his pocket, but he

forgot to have it filled. Every morning for two years, he showed it to the conductor as a railroad pass. Twice, it got him into the movies, once into the baseball park, and once into the symphony. He got a raise at work by showing it as a note from the boss.

One day, he mislaid it. His daughter picked it up, played it on the piano, and won a scholarship to a conservatory of music.

Not a True Story

The doctor was quite surprised when Humpty Dumpty came in for a checkup, but he went ahead anyway.

After he was done he said, "Well, Mr. Dumpty, I'm happy to tell you that those cracks will heal. But, I'm worried about your cholesterol levels!"

"Lose some weight, quit smoking, move around more, and eat the carrot."

16
My Body, Your Body, Every Body

Let's face it, bodies are embarrassing—and that makes them perfect fodder for jokes! But there's more to them than that. Big, small, wide, of whatever shape, our bodies are wonderful, intricate, complicated gifts from God. And we really ought to take better care of them.

We ought to, but. . .until we actually do there's some comfort to be had from the thought that other folk's bodies are as weird (and perhaps weirder) than ours!

If you have a poor body image remember you are a divine creation—and you're nowhere near as comical as this lot!

I Have a Hunch You Might Be Right

A hunchbacked man finally decided he needed to go to the doctor for a checkup. But right from the start he was reluctant to have the doctor look at him.

"I've been like this since school," he told the doctor. "I've hated people looking at me ever since."

The doctor reassured him that he might have been mocked for his appearance in the past, but for a doctor a hunched back was just another medical condition.

So the man took off his coat.

"You will have to take off a little more than that for me to examine you," the doctor said. So the man took off his sweater.

"A little more," the doctor encouraged. So the man took off his shirt.

"I will need to see you undressed," the doctor said. So the man reluctantly took off his undershirt.

"Tell me," said the doctor. "How long has it been since you attended school?"

"Twenty years," the hunchbacked man said. "Why?"

"Well," said the doctor, "did you never wonder what happened to your backpack?"

Not Recognized by the Manufacturer

Becky got hit by a car and was rushed to the hospital. It was touch and go. While on the operating table, she had a near-death experience. She saw God and asked, "Am I dead? Have you come to take me home?"

God said, "No, Becky, you have another forty years to live."

Afterward Becky decided to make the most of her stay in the hospital. She had collagen shots, cheek implants, a face lift, liposuction, and breast augmentation. She even had a hairdresser visit to dye her hair. She figured since she had another forty years, she might as well make the most of it.

Finally leaving the hospital Becky stepped onto the road and was hit by a car—again! This time she wasn't so lucky. And she wasn't best pleased when she saw God. "I thought you said I had another forty years?" she yelled.

"Becky?" God said. "Oh, wow! I didn't recognize you!"

Does It Hurt When I Do This?

A distraught woman went to see the doctor. "I hurt absolutely everywhere!" she said.

The doctor asked what she meant. To demonstrate she poked her side with her finger and yelled. "Oww!"

Then she poked her leg. "Ouch!"

She poked the palm of her other hand. "Ahhh!"

She poked her forehead. "The pain is just everywhere!" she cried. "What can I do?"

The doctor gave her a quick examination. Then he said, "Well, for a start you can stop poking yourself like that. You have a broken finger!"

You, Too, Can Be a Work of Art

While you are discussing any cosmetic procedure with your surgeon take a look at the artwork he hangs in his office. If it's Picasso or Dali—*run!*

Permanently Surprised

A cosmetic surgeon was asked if he had ever carried out any truly amazing procedures.

"No," the surgeon replied, a little grudgingly. "But I have raised a few eyebrows in my time."

I'm *Hearing* You, But. . .

A man's ears got badly frostbitten after he'd been ice fishing. A doctor told him it was okay, that he could have new ones grafted on. So he went in for surgery, and all seemed to go well.

But a week after he was discharged the man came storming into the doctor's office. "You gave me women's ears!" he yelled.

"Well, they are a bit petite," the doctor agrees, "but really, what's the difference?"

"I didn't notice any difference," the man said, "until I went for a beer with my friends— and not a single word they said made any sense!"

Beauty Is in the Eye of the Beholder— Unless the Beholder Is a Nurse

A woman went for her yearly physical, and the nurse took down her details.

"How much do you weigh?" the nurse asked.

"One hundred and ten pounds," the woman replied.

The nurse, who had been around the block a time or two, asked her to step on the scale. The woman weighed in at one hundred and fifty pounds.

"What height are you?" the nurse asked.

"Five feet eight inches."

The nurse measured her, and she turned out to be five feet four.

The nurse then checked the woman's blood pressure.

"It's really rather high," the nurse observed.

"Of course it's high!" the woman yelled. "When I came in here I was tall and slender, and now I'm short and fat!"

Veinity, Veinity, All Is Veinity

A woman entered a competition to see who had the most prominent veins. She didn't win but she came varicose!

It Should Be True

The latest scientific studies have found that pessimism is actually related to what blood type you have. The blood type of every single pessimist they examined was B-negative!

The Nose Have It!

You know, attitudes may be changing, but when it comes to cosmetic surgery a lot of people still turn their noses up!

Pick Up Thy Prescription—and Walk!

A man was waiting to have a prescription renewed, but the doctor was running late. So he contented himself with reading a few magazines.

When he was finally called in he stood up and discovered that because of the way he'd been sitting his left leg had gone to sleep.

He lurched forward, caught hold of the reception desk, limped his way along it, and then practically fell into the doctor's office. But sitting and talking to the doc for a few minutes allowed his circulation to get back to normal.

When he left the office with his prescription he was walking upright and straight. As he left the waiting room he heard one elderly lady whisper to her friend, "You see, Ellen! I told you he was a wonderful doctor."

Poor Sole!

A podiatrist opened a practice in a small town and happily cared for the feet of the residents of that town—until another podiatrist opened his practice right across the street!

From that moment on they were archrivals!

Break a Leg, Doc!

A doctor in a teaching hospital was discussing an x-ray with his students.

"This patient has been walking with a pronounced limp for some time," he said. "The x-ray shows us his fibula and tibia are radically arched."

He pointed to a student. "You. What would you do in this case?"

"Well, gee!" said the student. "I guess I'd limp as well."

Wherefore Art Thou, Corpuscle?

Once upon a time there were two red blood cells called Romeo and Juliette. They were completely devoted to each other, but sadly, their love was in vein.

We Go There for the Break

A man with a broken arm went to see the doctor.

"My goodness," said the doctor, "that's a bad break!"

"It's actually quite funny," the man said. "This is the third time I've broken my arm in the same place."

"Funny?" The doctor looked at the man as if he were mad. "You might want to think about not going to that place anymore!"

This Little Piggy Went for a Snooze

Q. Doctor, what do you call that feeling when your foot seems to go to sleep?

A. I do believe the medical term is "coma-toes."

The Secret of Antiquity

A doctor whose specialty was geriatrics spotted a wrinkled little man rocking on a porch swing. Something about him made the doctor want to talk.

"I couldn't help noticing how contented you looked there. Tell me, sir, what's the secret of your long and happy life?"

"Well," said the man. "I guess I put it down to smoking three packs of cigarettes a day, drinking a case of whisky a week, eating fatty foods at every meal, and never doing any exercise more strenuous than pushing this here swing."

"My goodness!" the doctor exclaimed. "Surely not! Tell me, what age are you?"

The man looked up, took a deep breath, and said, "Twenty-four."

Shut Up and Dance

Q. What do you get if you have strep throat on Friday?

    A. Saturday Night Fever.

If you enjoyed

Take Two Aspirin. . .and Call Me in Hawaii

be sure to check out

In the Marry Month:
The Best Wedding and Marriage Jokes and Cartoons
from The Joyful Noiseletter

Marriage offers endless opportunities for laughter—and this collection of wedding and marital humor, drawn from the files of *The Joyful Noiseletter*, is sure to please. Scores of jokes and humorous stories, all relating to the beloved institution of marriage, are categorized into chapters and accompanied by the cartoons of talented Christian artists. In the *Marry Month* is the first title in a planned quarterly release of joke books—arriving in plenty of time for the summer wedding season. This hilarious collection of marital mirth is ideal for couples, pastors, anyone looking for clean, good-humored content they can trust.

ISBN 978-1-61626-277-8 • Mass market paperback
192 pages • $4.99

Available wherever Christian books are sold.